DATE DUE			

Talking about Death

TALKING ABOUT DEATH

A Dialogue between Parent and Child

EARL A. GROLLMAN

**Third Edition
Updated and Expanded**

Drawings by Susan Avishai

BEACON PRESS   BOSTON

Beacon Press
25 Beacon Street
Boston, Massachusetts 02108-2800

Beacon Press books
are published under the auspices of
the Unitarian Universalist Association of Congregations.

97 96 95 94 93 92 91 90   2 3 4 5 6 7 8

Text design by Lisa Diercks

Library of Congress Cataloging-in-Publication Data
Grollman, Earl A.
Talking about death : a dialogue between parent and child / Earl
A. Grollman : drawings by Susan Avishai.—3rd ed., updated and
expanded.
p.   cm.
Includes bibliographical references.
ISBN 0–8070–2364–7
1. Children and death.   2. Death—Juvenile literature.   I. Title.
BF723.D3G72 1990
155.9'37—dc20   89–46061

To my future:

Jennifer Rebecca
Eric Paul
David Aaron
Samuel Isaac
Rebecca Rose

Contents

Preface

"I loved her so much. Why did she die?
Where does she go? Will I die, too?"

One of the most difficult problems for parents is helping a child through the crisis of death. Youngsters' feelings and perspectives are too often overlooked—an understandable response in our still death-denying, death-defying culture. The word DEAD has become the new four-letter word of pornography. Most parents today are convinced that they should be honest in discussing the biological processes of birth, but when it comes to life's end they may fall strangely silent.

In fact, most parents cannot recall how they told their children about the death of someone loved. The period surrounding the event becomes a blur. Adults struggling with their own grief do not believe a child can understand the tragic situation. A youngster's denial, silence, or sense of shock is too often taken to mean that the child does not understand that death has occurred and that children are not capable of mourning.

On the contrary. A child growing up today is more aware of the reality of death than you may realize. Grief is a deeply felt human emotion, as normal as playing, laughing, crying, or sleeping. Grief is a way of saying, "I miss you" or "I'm so sorry for all the things I've said and done." When you avoid children's reactions, you magnify their fears and replace reality with fantasy and psychological defenses.

This book is written with the hope that when death does occur, your child may be sympathetically guided toward an understanding of its real meaning. For the most effective results you could first read the section,

"A Parent's Guide to Talking about Death." Determine in advance the best method of interpreting the material: what points to emphasize, what lessons to be underscored. Those with religious convictions can supplement the discussion by sharing spiritual resources. In this dialogue, mention the specific name of the person who died.

When you read the book aloud, you may suddenly discover that you share the same emotions as those of the youngsters you're attempting to counsel. As Emerson observed in his journal, "Sorrow makes us all children again."

Finally, I would like to express my love and appreciation to my daughter, Sharon, for her creative and expert assistance in helping me revise this book.

Introduction

Youngsters continually encounter the fact of death in conversation and song as well as in the natural world of plants, animals, family, and friends. The question is not whether children should receive education about death, but whether the education they are receiving is helpful and reliable. Understanding death is a life-long process that continues from childhood through old age.

Of the many ways of dealing with death, the one most surely doomed to failure is the attempt to ignore it. Tell your children immediately about a death in the family; they should not hear the news from an acquaintance. Delay makes it all the more likely that they will be told by the wrong person in the wrong way.

Approach the discussion gently and lovingly; the tone of your voice should be warm, sympathetic, kind. *What* is said is significant, but *how* you say it will have a greater bearing on whether youngsters develop morbid fears or will be able to accept, within their capacity, the reality of death.

Before you share the "Read-Along" section with children, try to make sure that the house is relatively quiet and that there is ample time to be alone with them. It is neither necessary nor desirable to read the section in one sitting. Most youngsters could not possibly absorb all the information at once. Proceed gradually, according to their intellectual and emotional capabilities.

Pause from time to time to let them express what they feel and ask questions. Allow them to reveal their innermost fantasies and fears. "Will the person who died ever come back to life?" "Am I being punished because I did something wrong?'' ''Why didn't he even say good-bye to me?''

Permit them to vent the emotions of grief: anger, tears, guilt, despair, and protest are natural reactions to family disorganization. They may cry at nothing and laugh at everything. They may express hostility as well as affection. Grieving in *any* form is a necessary healing process.

You may be asked to repeat an explanation. Even an adult who first experiences a terrible crisis says, ''I don't believe it. It's a nightmare. It can't be true.'' So gently say it again. Denial is their way of coping with and working through a difficult situation. You may want to ask that they repeat what you have just explained.

On the other hand, a parent need not offer more information than the child is really seeking. A satisfactory response to the question ''What is death?'' should not be an involved theological or medical explanation but a simple, factual reply: ''A person does not breathe. The body is still, quiet, peaceful.'' Many parents project their own unresolved problems upon children. Over-answering reflects your own anxiety. A complicated answer results in confusion and distraction.

Children often mistake the meanings of words and phrases. I was once asked by a young girl, ''How long is death?'' I responded, ''Death is permanent.'' The youngster said, ''Oh, then it's not so bad.'' Noticing my bewilderment she said simply, ''My mother has permanents at the hairdresser. It doesn't last very long.''

Children often ask questions to test parents. Before answering, adults should try to explore the progression of thought that led to the child's inquiry. Otherwise, the reply could be misleading. When a boy was told that his grandfather died because he was old and sick, the child became preoccupied with his parents' health. He would cry whenever his mother or father had a simple cold. He discovered convenient reasons to stay away from nursery school and remain at home. ''How do you feel?'' he would ask again and again. His parents were irritated, not understanding that their son was convinced that their own death might soon occur. To the child, his parents were old as well as sick. What the boy needed to hear was that his parents' illness was different from that which caused the death of his grandfather, and that his parents would get better.

Don't tell your children what they will need to unlearn later. Avoid fairy tales and half-truths. Imaginative fancy only gets in the way when they are already having enough trouble separating the real from the make-believe. Youngsters need direct, simple, and honest age-appropriate information about death.

It is OK to admit that you don't have all the answers. There are no simple, foolproof answers to the mystery of death. Adults as well as children differ more widely in their reactions to death than in their re-actions to any other human phenomenon. There is no magic procedure that will comfort all people, either at the time of death or during the period that follows. Grief and adjustment do not work on strict time-tables. While one person will pick up the threads of life and work out new patterns relatively quickly, another will find, even after a longer period, little discernible movement toward a meaningful future.

While we all grieve at a different pace, almost all of us eventually go on with our lives.

Guidelines for Helping Children Who Have Experienced the Death of a Loved One

A Decalogue for the concerned parent

I. *Do* take the word "death" off the taboo list. Allow it to become a concept that can be discussed *openly* in the home, the school, the church, and the synagogue. The question is not whether children should receive death education, but whether the education they *are* receiving is helpful and reliable. Understanding is a life-long process that continues from childhood through old age. Death education begins when life begins.

II. *Do* understand that mourning and sadness are appropriate for people of all ages. *Children are people.* Grief now walks by their side. Numbness, denial, anger, panic, and physical illness are variations on their theme of pain. These are the normal, slow, winding avenues of sorrow and loss.

3

III. *Do* allow them to release their emotions. Let them call their feelings by the rightful names: "I am *angry*. I am *sad*. I am *hurt*." If they wish, they can scream it out. Or put their thoughts into words—in the form of poetry or a story. Or a song. Even a painting. It is not the *expression* of these legitimate emotions that is harmful, but their *suppression*.

IV. *Do* contact your children's school and inform them of the loss in the family; otherwise teachers might not understand any change in your youngster's grades or sudden sullenness or regressive behavior. When sensitive teachers share a problem with a child, they both establish a bond and help to relieve a burden.

V. *Do* seek help if you feel unable to deal with your children during this crisis. There are times when even the best-informed and well-intentioned adult is simply inadequate. Seeking further counsel from a clergyperson, child-guidance clinic, or therapist is not an admission of weakness but a demonstration of love and support. Sorrow leaves an imprint on the healthiest of personalities.

VI. *Do not* tell a child that he or she is now the man or woman of the house, or a replacement for a dead sibling. Never say, "You remind me so much of . . ." Do not treat your child as a substitute adult or surrogate relative, or as a friend . . . lover . . . companion . . . confidante. It is difficult enough for youngsters to lose a loved one. Do not deprive them of their childhood.

VII. *Do not* use stories and fairy tales as an explanation for the mystery of death. Never cover up the facts with a fiction or a confusing inter- pretation that you will some day have to repudiate. For example, to say, "Your father has gone away on a long journey" is to give the impression that he may someday return. If you say "God took your young mother because the Lord needs good people" you risk creating more confusion: good people *do* die young, but so do "bad" people. Children develop a deep resentment against a God who has capriciously robbed them of a mother whom they needed. Unhealthy explanations can create fear, doubt, and guilt, and encourage flights of fancy that are far more bizarre than reality. A child's greatest need is for trust and truth.

VIII. *Do not* let your children believe that you have all the final answers. Leave room for their doubts, questioning, and differences of opinion. Adults demonstrate their maturity when they say: "Are you surprised that I don't know everything about death? Don't be. That's why we need to talk together. Let's help each other." Respect their individuality, for in the long run they must find their own answers to the problems of life and death.

IX. *Do not* be afraid to express your own emotions of grief. If you repress your feelings, your children will be more likely to hold their own emotions at bay. Children receive permission to mourn from adults. A child can stand tears but not treachery; sorrow, but not deceit. To be able to show grief openly and to mourn without fear or embarrassment can help both children and parents to accept the naturalness and pain of death.

X. *Do not* forget to continue to give assurance of love and support. The greatest gift that parents can give a child is *themselves*. Their caring and concern over the next months and years will be of inestimable value in aiding recovery. Be willing to *listen* for minutes, hours, days. Youngsters need to talk, not just be talked to. Many children have an almost insatiable need to pour out their feelings.

Try to recall the wonderfully happy times shared together, not just the sad moment of death. Youngsters should be reminded that the loss of one important relationship does not necessarily mean the loss of others— including the one with you.

When words fail, touch! Attitude can be more important than words. Physical demonstrations of love and support are the greatest gifts to a grieving child. As you walk the long and difficult path of separation, you can find with your children new dimensions in their capacity for love, caring, and understanding. In truth, for people of all ages . . .

healing is a process,
recovery is a choice!

Children's Read-Along

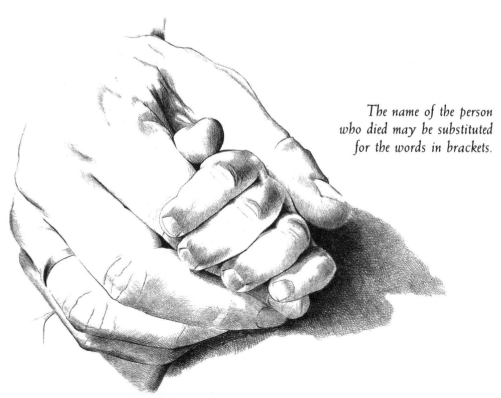

The name of the person
who died may be substituted
for the words in brackets.

When you die, you're dead.

Try saying that word, DEAD.

It's a hard word to say, isn't it?

Not hard to pronounce, really,
but hard to make yourself say.

Maybe because it's a sad word . . .
even a little frightening.

Let's say it again:

DEAD.

It's not like playing a game.

"Bang! I shot you! You're dead!"
And then you start all over again.

When people die,
they never come back to life again.

When people we love die,
we may want to pretend it didn't happen.

We don't want to believe it's true.
We think, "Maybe they'll really come back."

"Maybe the doctor was wrong."

"Maybe it was just a bad dream."

But we're only fooling ourselves.

When people die, we can't bring them back to life.

But what does "dead" mean?

Remember when we saw that animal that was hit by a car?
It was lying on the road . . .

still . . .

not breathing . . .

not moving . . .

its heart wasn't beating anymore.
The animal would never breathe or move again.

It was dead.

It's the same for people.

The body doesn't move.
It doesn't breathe.
The heart doesn't beat.

The body is still . . .
quiet and peaceful.

There is no hurt,
no pain, no life.

Like leaves that fall from a tree.

The leaves grow.
They turn colors,
and when it's almost winter
the leaves shrivel up.
They fall to the ground.

When a leaf dies, life has left it.

We can remember how beautiful it was,
but now it is dead.

"To everything there is a season
and a time to every purpose—

a time to be born, a time to die;
a time to cry and a time to laugh."

These words from the Bible tell us that for leaves,
and for all of us—for everything—
"There is a season,"
a time for every living thing to grow,

and then to die.

Just as there is joy in life,
there is also pain.

Just as there is happiness,
there are also tears.

When people we care about die,
we are sad.

We miss them so much
we may even cry.

What's wrong with that?

Nothing.

It's OK to cry.
It's our way of showing how sad we feel.

19

Are you worried?
Afraid you did something wrong,
and that [*the person we loved*] died
as a punishment to you?
OF COURSE NOT!

What you say or do or think cannot make people die.

You did nothing to make [*the person you loved*] die.
Let me say it again.

You did *nothing* to make [*the person you loved*] die.

Maybe you remember times you were mean.
Maybe you had angry thoughts or said terrible words.
But all people are like that sometimes.

We want to be good and loving,
but we don't always do the right thing.
What we say or do has nothing to do with
making a person die.

All people die.

Maybe you are angry that [*the person you loved*] died.

You might think:
Why is this happening to me?

Why did [*the person I loved*] just leave me
without even saying good-bye?

Maybe you feel left out and lonely.
A little hurt, maybe.

Is that how you feel?

Let's talk about it.

Do you want to tell me some of the things
that are troubling you?

Talking about them might help.

I will listen.

I will try to understand.
Like you, I am troubled and sad.
I am trying to find some answers, too.

Are you surprised that grown-ups
don't know all the answers about death?
Don't be.

No one really understands death,
but we can talk about it.

You can learn from me.

I can learn from you.

We can try to help each other.

When a person dies,
the people who loved them may come together
to remember.

Some may cry.

Sometimes, they may laugh, too,
as they remember the fun times
they shared together.

Just as it is OK to cry,
it is OK to smile and laugh.

Yes, we miss [*the person we loved*] so much.

We can no longer see them.

We can no longer talk to them.

But in a way they are still with us—
in our memories.

Tell me what you remember
about the fun things you did.

What made your times together special?

Do you remember the times [*the person you loved*]
made you so happy?

Now [*the person we loved*] is dead.

We are sad,
but we will always remember.

We can never forget the death,
but more important,

we will always remember the life and love
we shared together.

Parents' Guide to Explaining Death

This section elaborates on the questions children may have as you read the material on the preceding pages.

Explaining the Concept of Death

How Much Can Children Understand?

[Read-Along, page 9]

Can children actually understand death?

Many parents say, "Children are too young to understand. Why burden them with thoughts they cannot possibly grasp? Why not spare them adult grief?" But death is around your children all the time. Even at a very young age they are confronted with that inevitable moment when life no longer exists: a pet is killed; a funeral procession passes by; a public figure is assassinated; a grandparent dies; a space shuttle explodes; Bambi's mother is killed. And they see pictures of people being killed in vivid color on television.

What should you tell your children about the words DIE and DEAD? Your answers should correspond to the developmental age of your youngsters, the nature of the death, and their emotional involvement with it. Even children of the same age differ widely in their behavior and development: some are mature and stable even when faced with tragedy; others are seemingly immature and may seem younger in relation to their years. Remember that appearances can be deceiving. The child who seems to be the most collected may be most upset inside.

Do not try to fit your youngster's perception of death into a fixed age category. For every child, the meaning of death is reexamined as life changes. The concept of death undergoes a continuous process of maturation. The following guidelines should be viewed as *general*.

Although an infant may not have an understanding of the word *death*, babies and toddlers do react to loss. Changes in the emotional atmosphere of the home and the responses of significant others may upset the secure world of the child. Very young children may respond with irritability, variations in crying or eating patterns, and bowel or bladder disturbances.

Small children have a pervasive fear of being abandoned. Dr. Lester Grinspoon, in the August 1988 edition of the *Harvard Medical School Mental Health Letter*, writes: "The fear of separation from parents begins about the age of one and may last until seven or eight." After a death in the family, children with separation anxiety may be afraid to go to school, camp, or even sleep over at a friend's home. They frequently demand excessive attention from parents, cling to them, follow them around; even climb into their bed at night. They fear that if they become separated either they or their parents will come to harm. Some children are not able to concentrate on their activities, become withdrawn from their friends, and are generally apathetic and depressed.

Psychologist Maria Nagy researched one of the first and most comprehensive studies of children's perceptions of death. Her investigation found that youngsters have three recurring questions: What is death? What makes people die? What happens to people when they die; where do they go?

A preschool child may not believe that death is final. Death is like sleep: you are asleep, then you wake up. Or it is like taking a journey: you go away, and then you come back. A child experiences some aspects of what he or she considers "death" when father or mother goes to work. It is like playing "peek-a-boo" (an expression that comes from the Old English, meaning "alive or dead"). One moment you are here, then you are not.

The time concepts of the young are limited. Death is simply being less alive. Even after the funeral, parents may be shocked by the question, "When is Aunt Sara coming back?" Although the child may not fully understand your answer, your explanation should be, "Aunt Sara cannot come back because she is dead." Try to emphasize again and again in words that the youngster can understand that death is *not* a temporary phenomenon.

"Death is final," parents assert positively, but how can that be so? The child hears older siblings tell ghost stories in which spirits of the dead continue to live. A clergyperson's discussion of an afterlife suggests a return to life. The youngster watches a television program in which cartoon characters miraculously rise up again after being crushed or blown apart. Death and life seem interchangeable.

To many younger children, death is usually thought of as accidental. One dies when run over by a car or attacked by robbers. Death is often associated with violence, particularly dismemberment. Death is not inevitable—people may live forever if they are fortunate and careful.

Normal anxiety may be intensified, for example, fear of the dark, of going to sleep, of going to a new place, or of a parent going on a business trip. Youngsters often regress to a behavior that had been given up prior to the death, with a return to thumb-sucking or bed-wetting.

For those three- to four-year-olds who seem to believe in the interchangeability of life and death, or believe that the dead are "waiting to live in another place," parents must listen to the children's thoughts, concerns, images, and experiences. Hear their questions: "Do dead people eat the same kinds of food we do?" "Can they watch television?" "Can they talk to each other?" Repeat *again and again* that the person is dead and is not coming back to life and is not living in the cemetery. Explain that the death is not a punishment for bad behavior. Youngsters are rightly curious and anxious about death with its separation from familiar people and the anxiety, terror, and fear which that separation brings. And when words fail, touch them, hold them, show them your affection and love.

AGES FIVE TO NINE

Because of their life experiences, youngsters of this age are better able to understand the meaning of physical death. Death is final; living things must die. But they may not think of it happening to them. At this stage, they may neither deny death nor accept its inevitability. A compromise is made. Death is "real" but only for others; namely, the aged.

For some there is a strong tendency to consider death as a physical manifestation in the form of a person or spirit. One religious child conceived of an angel of death with long, fancy wings. Those who watch horror shows may believe death is a boogeyman, a skeleton, or a ghost that makes the rounds late at night and selectively carries away helpless victims. Children in this age range cope best when they receive simple, honest, and accurate information.

AGES TEN AND OLDER

Children at this stage are now able to formulate realistic concepts based on biological observation. Death is not a person but a perceptible end of bodily life. A dog runs into the street and is hit by a car. The animal can no longer get up to play. Dead is dead. It is final and universal. It is brought about by natural as well as accidental causes. Death is that inevitable experience which happens to all, including the child.

Death as the end of life is an especially frightening and painful event for young people ten years of age and older. Death is now a biological failure of organs to function. The magical, life-renewing conception of death is replaced by one that is terminal and fearsome. This perspective carries with it feelings of fragility as young people search for their own identity and philosophy of life and death.

When a loved one dies, children of this age may have difficulty in concentrating, exhibit a decline in the quality of their schoolwork, become withdrawn and isolated from family and friends, and seem persistently angry and sad. There could be frequent physical complaints with constant fatigue and frequent drowsiness. For older children, unresolved grief may be reflected in drug or alcohol abuse, impulsive behavior, and increased risk-taking. Instead of controlling their moods, their moods control them.

The way in which youngsters work through their grief depends a great deal on how family members and friends reach out to them. The more they are encouraged to share their grief, the more likely they will be better able to cope with the loss in their life. Grieving may help to bring direction to their lives as they become more open to others. "After this, I know I can handle anything," one youth said. "I now know that our family will stick together and who my real friends are. I'm able to remember the person who died without always crying by thinking of some of the great times we had together."

Being Honest about Death

[Read-Along, pages 14 and 15]

When a school nurse died, a teacher told the class: "I'm sorry to tell you, but we lost Mrs. Thompson." A student replied: "Don't worry. We'll find her."

People don't die. They "pass on," "pass away," "perish," "expire," "go away," "depart," or are "lost." Euphemisms get in the way of children's understanding as they attempt to distinguish reality from fantasy.

Often when you resort to euphemisms, you are deceiving yourself, not your youngsters. In a study entitled "Who's Afraid of Death on the Leukemia Ward?" Dr. Joel Vernick describes a concerted effort by the ward's staff to conceal the diagnosis from children. All the attempts to hush up the truth were in vain. Even the very young realized in some way that they were seriously ill and could die at any time. All parents should realize that it is almost impossible to deceive children.

Avoidance simply creates further anxiety. Ignorance about death can be terrifying and disruptive. The most daunting reality is better than uncertainty. I have seen people, when told that they had an incurable disease, breathe a sigh of relief and say, "I'm still frightened, but at least I know now what is really wrong with me." When you confront death, you begin to cope with the actualities of life. No one should be kept in emotional and intellectual isolation.

Evasion indicates your own inability to deal honestly with real situations. Where can one turn for help if no one will admit that there *is a*

39

tragedy? If loss can be acknowledged, you and your children may find comfort in what you can mean to each other—even in the midst of lingering pain and loneliness.

Death is a universal and inevitable process that must be faced by people of all ages. Children who are able to participate with their families after the death of someone they love will be better equipped to understand and manage the emotions of their grief. Your children are human beings, worthy of respect and openness, not pretense and equivocation. Two of their greatest needs are for *trust* and *truth.*

A woman's husband had just been killed in an automobile accident. How could she break the news to her four-year-old daughter? She said, "Daddy has gone away for a long time."

The girl became angry. Far from being comforted, she reacted with resentment and asked, "Why didn't he say good-bye?" Adults' reactions are similar—death is a kind of desertion. A widow may think, "How could he do this to me? Why did he leave me all alone?" Her euphemism for death is "when my husband *left me,*" as if it were a willful act.

Youngsters may develop a delusion that someday the father will return. After all, he has been away before and always comes back. Or they could unconsciously assume, "Daddy doesn't really care about me. He won't even write. Maybe I did something wrong and he is staying away to punish me." The deception is further compounded when the child thinks, "Why is everyone so sad because he went away for a while?"

To say to a child, "Your father went away on a long journey" is a way of providing temporary solace and easing the strain of the absence. But there is no point in saying something that youngsters must later unlearn. You are catering to misconception and fantasy.

There is no need to avoid the word DIE, especially since death is dramatized so frequently on television. A child will more readily understand a direct statement about death than some evasive term like "going away," which may lead to a fear that living people who go away may never return.

How Do I Start to Explain Death?

"I know that I should discuss death with my children. But to be honest with you, I'm confused myself. How would I begin?"

Do not begin by asking, "Have you ever thought what you will do when I die?" Such an introduction is security-shaking for both parent and child. Nor should an initial explanation be based on dogma, belief, or theology. Philosophical interpretations are too abstract for a child to comprehend.

Death and its meaning should be approached gently, indirectly, tenderly. An explanation might involve trees and leaves and how long they last. Point out to your youngster the diverse forms, shapes, and colors of nature, such as bugs, snails, butterflies. Once they moved; now are quietly still. Start with nonthreatening examples and proceed slowly, step by step, in accordance with the child's ability to understand.

Distinguishing Fantasy from Reality

[Read-Along, page 10]

When the space shuttle exploded, a younger girl didn't seem to be bothered by the tragedy. When an older child yelled, "Don't you care?" the young girl exclaimed: "Why are you so sad? They'll be back."

In some games, children shoot each other "dead." Then they start all over again and play another game. In the world of fantasy, youngsters pretend that a crisis never occurred. Or that they have a magical power to make the one who died come back to life. After all, many frightening fairy tales have happy endings. Good people are rewarded and live happily ever after. Sleeping Beauty marries a prince.

The very young attribute life to inanimate objects such as toys and playthings. One boy placed a marble in the sand and watered it in the belief that it would grow. Children need to understand that there is a difference between stuffed animals and real pets, between dolls and live babies; between human-made objects and living things. Puppets get broken; people die. Of all the creatures human beings are the only ones able to understand that they cannot live forever. An essential part of our humanity is that we find meanings for death as well as for life.

Children must learn that certain things in life cannot be changed; all of us must live with the given. Death is real. People who die are dead. They do not come back to life.

Explaining about Death and Illness

The grandmother died of a heart attack after a long illness. She had been in failing health for years. It seemed natural for the parents to explain, "Grandma died because she was sick."

People do become sick and die, but almost everyone who becomes ill survives. Youngsters may come to equate death with physical ailments—even slight ones—and hospitals. They think, "Will I die when I have the flu? What will happen when I go to the hospital to have my tonsils taken out?" Make a clear distinction between a very serious illness and a simpler one.

A child may be terrified that he or she will die of some sickness that "took" a loved one. "I feel like Grandma. My heart hurts me." Youngsters become preoccupied with the physical symptoms that terminated the other's life; in a process of identification they transfer the symptoms to themselves. It is necessary to repeat again and again, "Even though you and the person who died are in the same family, you are different individuals. I can truthfully tell you that you are in good health. You should live for many, many years." Children may also need to be reassured that their parents or other family members will not suddenly die; they will not be abandoned.

Explaining about an Afterlife

"We can't be selfish," the father said, seeking to ease his son's pain. "God was lonely and wanted Mommy in heaven."

The concept of heaven is difficult for a child to grasp. "But Daddy, if Mommy is going to heaven, then why are they putting her in the ground?" Some children peer from an airplane window seeking the loved one. Others hope rain coming down from heaven will bring the loved one back to earth.

You may feel that your own beliefs are too stark for a youngster—that it would be more comforting to express a religious conviction that you do not personally hold. So you spin out a tale of heavenly happiness while hopeless finality fills your own heart. You comfort the child by saying, "Mommy will always be with us," while you mourn that person as irretrievably gone. Children have built-in radar and quickly detect your inconsistency and deception. Share honest religious convictions, but be prepared for further questions concerning simplistic theological terms. Religious convictions *can* bring comfort and understanding to children if they are carefully explained.

Do not, however, paint too beautiful a picture of the world-to-come. Some children have attempted suicide in the hope of joining the absent loved one. By taking their own lives, they intend to restore the loss and at the same time be with God in Paradise.

"Isn't it beautiful! God chose Mark to be an angel because Mark was so innocent. God picks only the prettiest of flowers."

Despite good intentions, statements like these are a questionable religious approach to understanding death. *You* may understand that the "Lord giveth and taketh away" in the sense that God, who makes life possible, also makes death inevitable. But to assert that God wants the loved one "because the person was so good," or the "prettiest flower," denies the truth that *all* individuals die—the good and the "bad."

43

One little boy developed a deep resentment against a God who capriciously robbed him of someone he loved. To state that "God took him" or "God wanted him" could make God appear an enemy—vengefully striking the loved one down for being virtuous.

Some interpret a young person's death in a similar way. "God loves the young and pure." Nonsense! There is no causal relationship between longevity and goodness. Good people may die young, but they may also live to a ripe old age. One girl became so upset that she cried, "But I'm young and God loves me, too. Maybe I'll be the next one God takes away." To her, God became a vindictive figure, not a loving Deity. Suffering and death should not be linked with either sin and punishment or reward.

Is It Helpful to Compare Death with Being Asleep?

"Your grandma is dead now; she's gone to sleep for a long, long time."

It is natural to draw a parallel between sleep and death. In the *Iliad*, Homer alludes to sleep (Hypnos) and death (Thanatos) as twin brothers. Religious prayers often link the two words. Some people arise each morning and thank God for restoring them to life.

Be careful, however, to explain the difference between the two words; otherwise, you run the risk of causing a pathological dread of bedtime. Some youngsters struggle to stay awake all night because they fear that if they fall asleep they will never wake up again.

A familiar nursery prayer, which has alarmed some children throughout the ages, reads:

> Now I lay me down to sleep.
> I pray the Lord my soul to keep.
> If I should die before I wake,
> I pray the Lord my soul to take.

One little girl was convinced that God "killed" people during sleep. An enlightened writer has revised the bedtime prayer as follows, without anxiety-producing overtones:

> Now I lay me down to sleep.
> I pray the Lord Thy child to keep.
> Thy love guard me through the night
> And wake me with the morning light.

Linking death with sleep can also result in misunderstanding and denial. After all, if Grandpa is "sleeping," won't he wake up? A few misguided funeral directors have contributed to the avoidance of death by calling a room in the funeral home a "slumber room."

You must not respond to children with fiction and half-truths. Grandpa did not go on a long journey. He is not asleep. Loss is real; separation is painful; and death does indeed bring an end to life.

Death as Part of the Cycle of Nature [Read-Along, page 16]

Look in the woods. See those plants that are dying. Most of them will be dead before long. But look there. Other shoots are beginning to come up. Nature constantly renews itself. It's the same for people. Living and dying are part of human unfolding. Four billion of us are here on the planet Earth. Someday we will be no more. All things have a life-span—our bodies, trees, flowers, animals, and plants. Yet there will be other people, trees, flowers, plants to inhabit the world. Everything that is alive is the renewal of something that died, cell for cell. These are the cyclic rhythms of nature—night and day, phases of the moon, seasons, lives of insects, seeds, plants, animals, people.

Children understand the mystery of death through an exploration of nature—its diversity and its sameness, its dependability and its unpredictability, its beauty and its grotesqueness. There are changes and

45

growth each day from larva to butterfly, from egg to tadpole and frog. New leaves replace old ones that die.

A living tree produces seeds so that life may continue. Learning that death is part of life begins with the physical parting of the infant from the mother. While separation is sad and painful, it is an essential part of life and nature. "There is a time for every living thing to grow and to flourish and then to die" (Ecclesiastes 3:1).

[Read-Along, page 25] ## Being Honest about Your Limitations

"My children look up to me and respect me. God forbid that I should let them down and tell them that I, too, am confused over their aunt's death."

You do not diminish yourself in your children's estimation when you tell them you don't have all the answers. They probably reached this conclusion a long time ago. Adults are *not* all-powerful and all-knowing. You demonstrate maturity when you display honest uncertainty. It is far healthier for you and your children to seek understanding together rather than to attempt to protect parental authority with glib half-truths or evasions.

Don't be didactic; leave the door open. You might help the child struggle with the problem by saying, "Lots of people think about death in different ways. But no one has the final answers. Tell me what you think . . ."

Your children will both challenge and help you. In your quest to find answers for them, you may discover explanations for yourself. Their honest and direct doubts may compel you to come to terms with your own thoughts and feelings.

A wise person once said, "I have some good answers. Do you understand the real question?" Not all questions have final answers. Unanswered problems are part of life.

Understanding Your Children's Emotions

Denial
[Read-Along, page 13]

In the newspapers it was reported that when President Kennedy's son, John, returned on a visit to the White House following the death of his father and saw his father's former secretary, he looked up at her and asked, "When is my daddy coming back?"

Denial is a natural reaction to loss and takes many forms. In a state of shock the survivor says, "No, it's not true. It's just a terrible dream." One discusses the loved one in the present rather than the past tense. The room of the loved one is left intact in anticipation of return.

Denial is encouraged by silence and secrecy. Adults often insulate a child with the hope of protecting themselves as well as their youngsters from the pain of loss. In James Agee's novel *A Death in the Family*, the child, Rufus, senses the parent's unwillingness to discuss what has occurred:

> When you want to know more about it (and her eyes become still more vibrant) just ask me, just ask me and I'll tell you because you ought to know. "How did he get hurt," Rufus wanted to ask, but he knew by her eyes that she did not mean at all what she said, not now, anyway, not this minute, he need not ask; and now he did not want to ask because he too was afraid; he nodded to let her know he understood her.

Parents shape attitudes toward death for their children. It is natural to try to shield young people from pain. But you have learned that, just as you cannot protect yourself from life, so you cannot protect your youngsters from death. Traumatic experiences belong to both adulthood and childhood.

Young people have particular difficulty facing reality. I was once called to a home where a girl's father had just died. When the daughter returned home, she was told the sad news. Casually she said, "Oh, he died." Then she asked, after a pause: "Is it all right if I go out and play?" I considered the child to be uncaring and thought, "Didn't she really love her father?" It was not until later that I realized that the impact of death does not immediately penetrate the minds and hearts of survivors. For example, a most difficult time for bereaved people of all ages is not at the time of death, when they are surrounded by friends and family—it is months and even years later when they are able to realize the full impact of being alone. Children may grieve even longer than adults, but perhaps not initially, when there is still a sense of unreality about the death.

A child may look unaffected because she is trying to defend herself against the death by pretending it has not really happened. The parent may be relieved: "Isn't it lucky! I'm sure she misses her father, but she doesn't seem to be really bothered by it." A lack of response may signify that the child has found the loss too great to accept and pretends secretly that the loved one is still alive.

The fact that you and your children go through moments of denial need not indicate an abnormal mourning reaction. Your pain is momentarily forgotten. Then like a sudden storm, anguish floods in. Temporary forgetfulness enables a person to put aside the morbid, upsetting, and depressing aspects of death by focusing on the more constructive issues of the business of living.

Grief

[Read-Along, page 18]

"My daughter really surprised me when her friend died. She is such a young child, but she seemed more upset than most of the adults."

Grief is an expression of love. Mourning is an appropriate emotion for people of all ages. Children are no strangers to unhappy feelings—they know what it means to be mad, sad, guilty, afraid, lonely.

Children may experience three phases of a normal grieving process. The first is protest, when they cannot quite believe that the person is dead and they attempt, sometimes angrily, to regain him or her. The next is pain, despair, and disorganization, when youngsters begin to accept the fact that the loved one *is* really dead. Finally, there is hope when they reorganize their life without the person who died.

Children's responses to grief fluctuate according to their concepts of death, their developmental level, and the way they related to the person now dead. Some will not speak about the individual who died; others will speak of nothing else. Some will talk of the death at unexpected times—months or even years after the person has died. Some will cry hysterically; others will remain outwardly impassive and emotionless; others may even laugh. Some will praise the deceased as the most wonderful person in the whole world; others will hate the individual for leaving them alone and abandoned. Some will blame themselves for the death; others will project their grief upon God, the physician, the clergy, the funeral director, or members of the family. Children's despair may be interrupted by a carefree mood, vacillating between sadness and playful joy. Reactions are varied and contradictory, often unpredictable.

Youngsters should not be deprived of the right to grieve. They should no more be excluded from sharing grief and sorrow than they should be prevented from demonstrating joy and happiness. Each person should be given the opportunity to lament the end of life in his or her own way.

Crying

[Read-Along, page 18]   *"Show me what a grown-up you are. Be brave. Don't cry."*

But crying is a natural emotion. A newborn enters life crying for more oxygen. In early life, tears are an infant's means of expressing needs, pains, and discomforts. Even after children are able to verbalize their desires, they continue to weep in order to release painful emotion.

Tears are a tender tribute of yearning affection for those who have died but are not forgotten. Weeping helps to assuage heartache—to express that inevitable depth of despair that follows the slow realization that the death is not a bad dream.

Do not be afraid of causing tears; they are like a safety valve. Often people deliberately turn a conversation away from loss. They are apprehensive of the weeping that may follow. They do not understand that expressing grief is normal and helpful.

Children should never be discouraged from crying to express their grief. Why should they be forbidden from expressing inner feelings? They loved the person who died. They miss the individual. And they too need to relieve painful emotions.

Only an uninformed adult would say of children who have experienced tragedy and remained dispassionate, "The youngsters are taking it so well. They never cry." The old bromide, "Be brave!" encourages children to bottle up true feelings and minimize their loss. Children who stoically repress grief may later find release in an explosion more dangerous to their inner makeup.

Do not feel that you have failed when you weep in front of your child. The opposite is true. It expresses the undeniable fact that you too are human and need emotional release. It is better to say, "I have been crying, too" rather than, "There, there, you mustn't cry." Some of the most tender experiences I have witnessed are parents and children weeping together and sharing the real meaning of the pain of separation.

In our culture, the gift of tears seems to be reserved for one sex: crying is mistakenly considered a female trait. This lesson is first demonstrated when a little boy falls off a swing, bumps his head, and out of fright and hurt begins to cry. The mother or father quickly runs out of the house, picks him up, and says, "Quiet, big boys don't cry." The truth is that all people, regardless of age or sex, simply feel better after a good cry.

While you should not deny a youngster the opportunity to weep, neither should you urge the child to display unfelt feelings. Children should not be subjected to emotional blackmail in which they are urged to behave in some particular manner, such as remaining still when they need to run and jump. Each child reacts differently. Some children need to cry freely. Others may be able to get by with a few tears. There are some who may not weep at all for a loved one who lived far away and did not touch the child's life. Youngsters feel confused and hypocritical when told to express sentiments they do not honestly feel. There are other outlets for emotion besides tears. Allow them to express those feelings that are appropriate to their needs.

Anger

[Read-Along, page 22]

"Sometimes I hate my sister for dying. Nothing's the same anymore. She's ruined everything."

From denial—"No, not me"—children may turn in anger and ask, "Why me?" The bereaved are often bitter and resentful for their misfortune; they may become irritable and difficult to manage. The sense of helplessness turns to bitterness.

A first impulse of an enraged individual is to lash out at the people who are perceived as having caused the suffering. It is natural to wish to retaliate against those who have hurt you. Adults understand this need to vent their hostility, yet often they won't tolerate this behavior in their children.

Do not react to your children's anger with threats of further punishment. They have enough guilt and pain. Instead, approach them with patience and respect. Listen as they tell you about their fears and ani-

51

mosity. If you say, "How can you speak about your poor, dead sister that way?" you bring the dialogue to a speedy and unsatisfactory conclusion.

Never scold them for feelings, or make them feel ashamed of their emotions, or tell them that they should have only good thoughts about the person who has died. If you and your child cannot recall unhappy memories of the deceased, then you may not yet have accepted the reality of death.

Resentment is a natural part of the grieving process and helps to express anguish and frustration at the curtailment of a life so precious. Bottling up anger causes greater stress and leads to depression.

[Read-Along, page 21]

Guilt

A mother said to her son: "You keep your bedroom like a pigsty. You will be the death of me yet." The mother died shortly thereafter. The boy suffered terrible guilt because he believed his sloppiness was the cause of her death.

There is a degree of guilt involved in almost every death. It is human to blame yourself for past failures. Adults who do everything in their power to make a loved one happy may search for ways they should have done more. After a plane crash, one man could not stop condemning himself for having quarreled with his wife just before her untimely death. Recrimination is an attempt to turn back the clock, undo the wrong things for which the survivor now feels guilty, and somehow magically restore the loss.

Guilt takes many forms. It can be directed outwardly through aggressiveness and hostility: "Daddy, why didn't you call the ambulance in time? If you had, Mommy would be alive today!" By projecting guilt upon someone else, youngsters absolve themselves from blame. Guilt may be turned inward and cause depression. Children may be unable to concentrate on schoolwork. They may become too preoccupied with a sense of failure to join others in play. Some cannot sleep, and when they do, have recurrent nightmares. Unresolved grief also takes the form of withdrawal, delinquency, excessive excitability, self-pity, and defiance.

Children are more likely to feel guilt than adults. In their experiences, bad things happen when they are naughty. If your son gets good grades in school, he is rewarded. On the other hand, when he hits his sister, he may be punished by losing television privileges. The "desertion" of a loved one must therefore be a retribution for wrongdoing. He searches his mind for the "bad thing" for which he is being penalized. Adults experience the same process. After a death, every clergyperson has heard the question, "Why am I being punished?"

From a commonsense point of view, a youngster's guilt may seem unreasonable to the parents. Yet pangs of guilt are agonizing, even when induced by a misconception of reality. One girl was told that in order to live she must eat. Since she did not eat her cereal the morning her father died, she concluded that she must be responsible for his death.

Parents may inadvertently create guilt by not explaining facts or by inventing fictions. A college student reminisced about returning home from school when he was a first-grader to learn that his older sister "had gone away and would not come back." "Where did she go? What happened?" he inquired. "Don't ask so many questions" was the only response. For years he suffered recriminations, convinced in his own mind that he must have done something terrible to cause her disappearance. His guilt was only relieved when he took a course on dying, death, and bereavement at the university.

Young people believe in the power of magic, that, in the words of an old song, "wishing makes it so." When one girl, angry with a friend, thought to herself, "How I hate him—I wish he would die" and the friend later *did* die, she felt accountable for the death.

The living may feel guilty simply because they are alive. This has been labeled "survivor's guilt." Perhaps they consider themselves censured for having wished that a sick person would hurry up and die. One thinks or says about the terminally ill, "It's enough. She is suffering so much. Why can't she go quickly and peacefully?" Then after death, one may be guilt-stricken for having wished that the afflicted individual could die with dignity and without pain.

Let children understand that nothing they did, said, or thought had anything to do with the death. You might emphasize, "Perhaps you were naughty at times. But nothing you did or thought makes a person die."

[Read-Along, page 28]

Remembering the Past

"I just can't wait to move out of the house. Every place reminds me of my child. It will be better for everyone if we just go away as far as possible."

A desire to run away is natural. Your heart is heavy with the thought that the past can never return. Then you realize that there is no escape. Your memories cannot, and should not, be denied. Ask yourself, "Why should I forget?" Although we are children of today and tomorrow, we are also children of yesterday. The past travels with us and makes us what we are. There is no love without loss, no joy without sorrow.

Don't make any abrupt, final decisions. Too many people have left the security of familiar surroundings only to discover that problems were intensified rather than diminished. Children especially need to retain roots in the same neighborhood with longtime playmates. Do not attempt to eradicate the memory of your loved one. Pictures are helpful for remembrance. Children may wish to be surrounded by some tangible reminders. They love mementos. One young girl was so delighted with her grandmother's hand mirror that she treasured it for the rest of her life.

Some people mistakenly believe that they are most helpful when they talk about every subject *except* the death that has taken place. Encourage what Sigmund Freud called the "ties of dissolution"—that is, recall with your child both pleasant and unpleasant memories. As each incident is reviewed, you feel anguish that an experience can never be repeated. But as the pain is lived through, you gradually untie emotional bonds.

Hear what your children are really saying. If you tell your friends you won the sweepstakes and they quietly say, "So what?" you are justified in thinking they care little about you. The same is true when a bereaved person asserts, "I really feel guilty." I should have been kinder and more compassionate," and all you can reply is, "Just don't think or talk about it." Cultivate the art of listening with a "third ear." Concentrate not only on what is being said, but also on the emotions behind it. Understand what your children need to express and what they seek to know.

Your children are working through the grieving process when there is the painful acceptance of the reality of death, when they reorganize their life around new circumstances, and reestablish normal relationships and activities. And always, they need your physical demonstrations of love and support.

Being Honest about Your Own Emotions [Read-Along, page 25]

"When my husband died, I didn't want my children to see me moping around the house. You just don't go around crying in front of your own kids."

As a member of the clergy, I used to think I too had to keep a "stiff upper lip." My role was to comfort others. I thought, "How would it look if I displayed weakness?"

I believed this for many years. I did not understand that what I had mistakenly labeled "weakness" was really being human. Because I was in the same congregation for more than a third of a century, I developed strong emotional bonds with many members. No longer do I attempt to stoically repress my feelings. On occasion I weep with the people I am consoling—for I, too, loved the person who died. My display of emotion has not diminished the survivors' esteem. On the contrary, on more than one occasion I heard the remark, "If the rabbi can shed a tear, why then is it so wrong for me?" If it is therapeutic for people to grieve for a loss, should professionals be exempt? Physicians, nurses, social workers, clergy, funeral directors—please take note: honestly felt emotions *may* be expressed.

When you mourn, you give children a model to follow. They understand that it is acceptable for their emotions to be out in the open. If you do not grieve, they may invent reasons for your lack of feeling: "Mommy isn't even crying. She probably didn't love Daddy." Or "Mommy is so jumpy lately. She must be angry at me for something I did." It is helpful to call an emotion by its rightful name: "I am ANGRY . . . SAD . . . HURT."

Avoiding feelings does not make them go away. Denial drives suffering inward, where it later emerges in a disguised or undesirable reaction. Don't you really feel better when your thoughts are expressed? "Did you know that I, too, am troubled?" Grief is worked through when *both* child and parent understand and reveal their uncomfortable feelings.

What Happens to the Person Who Died?

Explaining about a Funeral

"Of course, our children shouldn't go to the funeral. They're much too young."

The funeral is a rite of separation—the bad dream is indeed real. The presence of the casket actualizes the parting experience, transforming the process of denial to an acceptance of reality. It is an opportunity to say good-bye. The one who died will no longer be part of the familiar environment.

Yes, the funeral may be sad. But sadness is an integral part of the life cycle. Mental health is not the denial of tragedy, but the frank acknowledgment of it.

Youngsters cannot and should not be spared knowledge about death. When death occurs within or close to a family, no amount of caution and secrecy can hide from the children the feeling that something important and threatening has occurred. They cannot avoid being affected by the atmosphere of grief and solemnity. All the emotional reactions that youngsters are likely to have to a death in the family—sorrow and loneliness, anger and rejection, guilt, anxiety about the future, and the conviction that nothing is certain or stable any more—may be considerably lessened if they feel that they know what is going on and that you are not trying to hide things from them.

You might ask, "Do you think the children should attend the funeral service? They loved her very dearly. But I'm afraid that if they go, they will become disturbed. Wouldn't it be much better if they stayed with a friend on the day of the funeral?"

You may expect an affirmative reply, for you intend it as a kindness when you shield them from death. Yet recognized authorities have come to the conclusion that not only is it correct to permit children to attend a funeral, but that if they are old enough to go to church or synagogue, can understand what is taking place, and are able to sit through the service, they should be offered the opportunity of *participating* in a ceremony of farewell for the loved one.

Unfortunately, many adults project their own unresolved grief onto their children. For youngsters the funeral is not necessarily bizarre and strange. A child accepts the funeral rites as a natural way of paying respect. After all, death is no stranger. In school, they participate in the burial of a hamster. They witness the funerals of notables during television news programs. Children love pageantry. What is a funeral but a family ceremony?

The importance of the funeral ritual is dramatically portrayed in the French film *Forbidden Games.* A girl's parents are killed in an air raid. Thereafter she derives comfort from constantly playing "the game of funeral," giving a dead creature an elaborate interment with casket and flowers. Her game helps her to relive, digest, and ultimately master the shock of her parents' death.

Being denied the opportunity to say good-bye may harm even older children. Sometimes children away from home cannot be contacted for a parent's or grandparent's funeral. I have noticed time and again in such situations that these young people deny the reality of death when they return home. They were not given the opportunity of saying good-bye. That's why I recommend that older children come to the cemetery for a private service of farewell. Incompleted grief contributes to emotional illness. Therapists suggest that mourning rituals help initiate and catalyze hidden and unresolved grief problems.

You need not wait for an actual death before you explain the meaning of a funeral. In my own synagogue, a funeral director is invited to explain how a funeral *may* be conducted. (I emphasize the word *may* because each funeral is indeed different, expressing the needs of individual family members.)

Explain the purpose of the funeral and how it touches people on different levels. For the religious there is the sharing of spiritual values. However, the funeral is more than a religious event; it is much more than the practical and legal disposing of a human body. *A funeral is for the entire community to confer group strength.* You are not alone: one touch of sorrow makes the whole world kin. You are helped from the disorganized state of shock and guilt and grief through the valley of shadow. Your loved one has died, but friends and family still remain.

Discuss with your children what they might expect at the funeral. Explain that it will take place at a funeral home or church or synagogue. The clergyperson will read appropriate prayers. Perhaps the minister will talk about how the person who died touched our lives. The discussion of the things that counted in the loved one's life will be brought out in word and song and ritual. Point out that it can be a strengthening and sharing experience for the entire family.

People may cry. But, as we said, what's wrong with that? It's all right. It is one of our ways of showing how much we miss that person and wish to have him or her back. A purpose of the funeral is to provide a way for expressing grief.

When your youngsters understand what is occurring, they may be more relaxed about the unfolding events. It is easier for them to understand being *in*cluded than *ex*cluded, and they are far better off observing the funeral than living with fantasies conjured up by young and fertile imaginations.

It is difficult to determine whether youngsters should be encouraged to attend a funeral. Smaller children could disrupt the service. If they do attend, familiar adults should sit with them near the aisle, and be prepared to leave if necessary. Allow those older children to decide whether they wish to attend.

Very often it is the parents who unconsciously make up the children's minds, saying, "You don't want to go, do you?" The decision is made not only in words but by the tone of voice. After hearing what they may expect at the ceremony, youngsters may change their minds many times. If the judgment is not to attend, do not place any shaming pressure upon them. You may certainly suggest that perhaps later you may visit the cemetery together.

Don't arbitrarily send children to stay with friends or relatives. They might construe the dismissal as another kind of abandonment or rejection. Let them know that, if they desire, you would be pleased to have them with you. Their presence could be a comfort at this difficult time. Some enlightened adults have helped youngsters feel that they have an important role to play by asking them to answer the doorbell and telephone. They are given the opportunity to mingle with the family and feel needed.

Just as your children cannot be spared knowledge about death, they cannot and should not be excluded from the grief and mourning following death. They too have both a right and a need to say good-bye.

What Happens after the Funeral

A child asks her father as they drive by a cemetery, "Daddy, what's that place we're passing?"

"You're too young to understand. I'll explain it to you when you're older."

Usually, the first question a child asks when someone dies is, "Where is she now?" Those with a religious orientation can state their belief, but there is another answer that many can give: a factual one. You could say, "When she died her body was placed in a casket and buried in the earth. A stone or plaque will show where she is buried. People can come to the grave to say a prayer or just to think about the person."

Of course, not all people are buried in the earth. Some are put above the ground in a mausoleum, a building with spaces cut in the wall for crypts or vaults for the casket. And for still others, the body is burned in a place called a crematory. The ashes may be placed in a small box or urn. Or the ashes can be scattered over the ground or the ocean. Above ground, the box or urn is deposited in a space in the wall of a building called a "columbarium." These technical terms, however, are unimportant. What is significant is your honest, informative answers to their question.

Don't wait until a person dies before you visit a cemetery. When you drive by a burial ground and your child asks, "What is that?" you might stop to walk through together. It is not really so traumatic for the youngster. Mystery is finally removed; shadowy ghosts are replaced by real understanding.

If children do not attend the interment service, they may come to the cemetery later with their family. This is advisable when a child cannot accept the reality of death. One boy was told that his mother "went on a journey." Thereafter he became sullen and unmanageable. Whenever his mother's name was mentioned, the child would speak of her in vile language. Then finally one day the child was told the truth. He was taken to the cemetery where he could visit the grave. The child was heartbroken, for he now realized that she had really died. Yet he also felt comforted, for he now knew what had happened. And most important, he knew that his mother had not run away and abandoned him.

A funeral does not end in the funeral home or church or synagogue. Its logical conclusion is the grave, the mausoleum, or the columbarium where the loved one is placed. This is where the person is buried.

How Children React to Specific Kinds of Death

The Death of a Parent

"Since my husband died, my daughter just can't seem to find herself."

One of the greatest difficulties for a child is the death of a parent. The world will never again be as secure. Youngsters are deprived of attention and love they desperately need and want. "Who will take care of me now?" "Suppose something happens to you, Mommy?"

In her book *How It Feels When a Parent Dies*, Jill Krementz talked with eight youngsters ranging in age from seven to sixteen. One child told her: "When Mom told me that Daddy was dead my knees started shaking. I almost fell down. My sister Peg screamed when she found out. My hands still shake when I think about my father." Another whose mother died had nightmares: "I had a dream that she was lying at the bottom of a closet and she came back to life. When I have dreams like that, I just pinch myself on the arm to see if I'm awake or dreaming."

The death of a parent affects each child differently. Anna Freud points out that a child's love for a mother becomes a pattern for all later loves: "The ability to love, like all other human facilities, has to be learned and practiced." If this relationship is interrupted through death or absence, the youngster may do one of four things: remain attached to a fantasy of the dead person; invest that love in things (or work); be frightened to love anyone but himself or herself; or accept the loss and find another person to love.

Often the surviving parent may inadvertently contribute to children's difficulties. Deprived of a mate, the parent may attempt to fill that empty space through total devotion to the youngsters. Avoid the temptation of making the child a surrogate partner. Your youngster must not replace the absent mate. Physical intimacy such as sharing a bedroom should be tactfully avoided. Potentially seductive and sexually stimulating situations can be even more damaging to your child. The child is not your lover, companion, confessor, or spouse. Children should be accepted within the confines of their psychological and intellectual capabilities and limitations. They are still youngsters and have their own difficult grief reactions to a parent's death to deal with.

The manner in which children cope with their loss depends a great deal on how the surviving parent behaves. If the parent acts as though life is completely unchanged, confused children will try to mimic that attitude, even though the result for the child will be greater insecurity. If the adult response is hostility, intense anxiety, or erratic behavior, youngsters may react similarly. If the response is a grief mingled with consistent, loving reassurance, children gain the confidence to handle the conflicts and changes they are experiencing.

Admittedly, it is difficult for the surviving parent to sustain a sense of family stability. How is one to cope with the personal loss, much less the kids? Again, there are support groups and professional counselors to help both parent and youngsters. No matter how consumed you are in your personal hell, it is important to give attention to the bereaved child. Following the death of a parent, youngsters will often be worried by three basic questions, which you should try to answer: Did I cause this to happen? Will this happen to you? Who will take care of me now?

If both parents die, special intervention is needed to help the children cope with their multiple loss. Let them know openly and honestly *where* they will be living and *with whom*. Whenever possible, allow them to participate in important decisions. Give them a listening ear, support, and encouragement. Often it is a close relative who assumes responsibility for the youngsters, but whoever does so, the surrogate parents must assist in helping the youngsters through the complex grieving process. Try not to make changes too quickly, for consistency is all-important in the children's changing world. The more freely youngsters are able to express feelings about the past and explore their concerns for the future, the more rapidly they will be able to work through their tremendous loss.

The Loss of a Brother or Sister

"Now that the older child has died, the younger one just doesn't seem the same anymore."

Children are not supposed to die. They are expected to live long productive lives and grow into old age. In the words of the Society of Compassionate Friends, "There is no death so saddening as the loss of your beloved child." Parents may not be able to maintain a healthy relationship with each other because they feel helpless and disturbed. It is estimated that three-quarters of the couples who experience the death of a child separate or divorce.

Not only parents but siblings as well may be thrown into crisis. It is difficult to witness parents' anguish and inconsolable pain. Support for young people is often minimal because family and friends are concerned almost solely with the adults. Youngsters are justifiably frightened because it seems as if life will never again be normal and happy.

Children's reaction to the death of a sibling may be the realization that it could happen to them. After all, they are part of the same biological inheritance. "Is something also wrong with me?" they may wonder. "Will I die when I reach my brother's age?" Youngsters may assume babyish behavior to magically prevent themselves from growing old and dying. (Parents should say again and again, "You are fine. There is nothing wrong with you. You do not have the disease that caused your brother's death.")

Seeing the grieving parents, a child may try to "replace" the brother or sister and make everything all right again. Adults sometimes unconsciously promote this kind of behavior by saying, "You know, you are so much like him in so many ways." Parents who do this are only hurting themselves and their living children. As difficult as it is to accept, you must now understand that one of your youngsters *is* dead. The child cannot be resurrected in the form of someone else. Let the dead lie in peace. Do not make comparisons. Your living child has enough difficulties without having to assume a new identity.

Surviving children are often beset with guilt. They remember the times when they fought and argued with the dead sibling. They recall past anger and jealousy. "Is death a punishment for my being bad?" they may wonder. Listen to your youngsters' fears and feelings.

The following responses reveal the innermost thoughts of a group of young people who attended a 1986 meeting of Compassionate Friends:

When my sibling died I felt:

- that a part of me died and that I was all alone.

- very angry at everything.

- that my childhood had died, too.

- angry and sad that my family life as I had known it was over.

- terrified that I would lose someone else that I loved.

- cheated that I didn't have a brother.

- that I wanted to cry.

- that I wanted him back.

When my sibling died, some problems I had were:

- Most people thought that my parents were the only people suffering.

- I was afraid to cry in front of my parents because I didn't want to upset them.

- People thought I should be over my grief in a week.

- I felt guilty when I felt happy about something.

- People refused to talk to me about the death of my sibling because they thought I might go crazy.

- People asking me how my parents are doing and not bothering to ask me how I'm doing.

- People saying it was only a brother or sister you lost and you shouldn't feel as bad as if you had lost your parents.

- Parents yelling at you because you don't show any emotion about your sibling's death and so they think that you don't care at all.

- People saying that they knew exactly how you felt when it had never happened to them.

- People expected me to be back to normal after a short time and didn't understand when I wasn't.

- My parents tended to get overprotective of me.

I find it hard to talk to my parents about the loss of my sibling because:

- I don't want to upset them.

- I hurt more when they hurt.

- I hate to see my mother cry.

- I would rather grieve by myself and keep it to myself.

- I don't get along with my mother that well.

- I fought with my sibling so often.

Parents must be attuned to the ambiguity of their children's feelings—sadness over loss, relief that a competitor is gone, anger over being left out, fear that they are now vulnerable to death. Remember that the death is a major tragedy in their life as well as yours. They, too, have suffered the loss of a playmate and companion, someone who was both dearly loved and resented as a rival. If the death followed a long illness, the surviving sibling may have endured months of neglect. Surviving children's ability to cope with their pain will be powerfully influenced by how parents and others understand their loss and express their grief *together*. Even though a terrible death has occurred, you are still a family. Your love for one another is not lost.

When a Friend Dies

When a junior high school student was diagnosed as having a terminal illness, the principal shuddered: "What do I do now?"

Glenn, an eighth-grader, was diagnosed with leukemia. The principal decided to share this information with his classmates. They needed to know why Glenn wore a baseball hat to cover his bald head and why his attendance at school was sporadic. Later the principal remarked: "Now that they understood the situation, the kids were wonderfully understanding. When Glenn was hospitalized there was a rush of cards and visits from many friends. Conversations were the normal chatter—what was happening in the Boy Scouts, who had troubles in school, and the latest baseball scores."

Glenn died. Immediately afterward, the principal met with each class and told them the sad news and that they had a right to grieve in the way that was appropriate. He alerted the faculty to be available to the students "since death would be a very important topic on their minds."

Forty percent of the students elected to go to the funeral. Many wrote personal letters to Glenn's family and interspersed their remarks with anecdotal material. In the ensuing days, teachers held small discussion groups for those pupils who wished to express their feelings both about Glenn and about the subject of death in general. Some talked about the injustice of Glenn's dying, how hard and how long he had suffered, and their own fears about death.

After the funeral, the principal, the school nurse, the physical therapist, and some of Glenn's classmates visited his family. Glenn was dead, but community support was desperately needed. "Our conversations were never long but we hoped our visits would help the family feel that the school cared about the living and that Glenn was not forgotten."

The death of a friend can have a ripple effect. Children suddenly become aware of their own mortality and realize that they too can die. Some fear that they might have "caught" the illness. One youngster had a fight with a student who was later killed and felt he was in some way responsible for the death. Children who have witnessed the death of a classmate may also have difficulty in returning to the place where the death occurred.

In the classroom, teachers, parents, and other concerned adults can help children understand what has occurred by discussing the reason for the now empty chair. Children may express their feelings verbally or through pictures and dramatic play. They can commemorate the event by dedicating the yearbook to the student's memory, or planting a tree, or placing a bookshelf in the school library. Parents and teachers must remember that effective grief work is not done alone, and that the way *out* of grief is *through* it.

When Suicide Occurs

"My husband took his life. Our son keeps saying, 'Maybe Daddy was angry with me.' "

Surviving children of a suicidal parent have special problems in coping with the tragedy. The statement, "You did nothing to make him die . . . all people die," could appear hollow. Of course everyone eventually dies. In the case of suicide, however, the person *deliberately* took his or her life. There is a far greater burden of guilt and anger. Because of the stigma, youngsters may carry the bitter experience for the rest of their lives.

The child may ask, "What did I do wrong? Did he commit suicide because I was bad and mean to him? Didn't he love me enough to want to live?" Death by suicide represents the greatest of all affronts to those who remain behind.

It is no help to say, "Don't talk about it." The child is going through an intense emotional crisis. He or she needs to articulate and act out reactions—denial, then bewilderment, and finally the weeping, despairing confrontation with the truth of the suicide. The bereaved need to pour out their hearts.

A most important way you can encourage their grief work is by listening responsively. For example, your son may tell you that he was cast in the same mold as the parent. He constantly recalls similarities, how they resembled one another both physically and mentally. Help the youngster understand the truth. There is no cruel seed of self-destruction lurking in him. The person who died is not the same person as the child who is beside you. Each individual is different. Suicidal tendencies are not bequeathed like family heirlooms.

Nor does it help to say that the one who took his life must have been out of his mind. The term "crazy" does not lighten the blow. The majority of persons who commit suicide are tormented but *they are not necessarily insane*. Telling survivors that the deceased was out of his mind does not comfort them; it only raises the fear of inherited insanity. The child may think, "I am his child; I must be crazy, too."

You might add, "There is much that we don't know about suicide. At that moment, death was his way of handling the troubled life. But you are not your father. Suicide is not inherited. You will learn that there are other ways to work through problems."

One of the nation's foremost death educators, Dr. Robert G. Stevenson of River Dell Regional Schools in Oradell, New Jersey, has enunciated some significant guidelines in helping survivors of suicide:

• Assist the bereaved to clarify their thoughts and feelings.

• Put an end to unfounded rumors that cause unnecessary additional pain.

- Don't romanticize the suicide by saying that he or she is "better off."

- Commemorate the death by perhaps attending the funeral and allowing the survivors to sense your continuing friendship and support.

- Help the bereaved by recalling the complete person with human strengths as well as weaknesses.

Neither parents nor children can control what has happened in the past, but you can take charge of how you will respond in the present. You can build the temple of tomorrow's dreams upon the grave of yesterday's bitterness.

The Death of a Pet

"Why are you crying so hard? It's only a dog. It's not as if something happened to your parents. We can always buy another pet."

When a pet dies, your children come face to face with the finality of death and the grief it brings. Your youngsters and the pet played together so often and now the fun is ended. Often the death of a pet may be a child's first introduction to a real death.

Children may mourn more deeply for a pet than for a human being. There is more irony than humor in the story of a mother who said, "David, I don't know how to say this. Your doggie died." David did not seem too disturbed, so the mother thought her son had not heard her. She repeated her statement. David then became visibly shaken. "Oh, no, don't tell me . . . I can't believe it. Tell me it isn't true. It's not so, is it?" The mother answered, "But I told you before and you acted so well. Why are you taking it so hard now?" David replied, "I didn't know my *doggie* died—I thought you said *Daddy* died."

The burial of a pet gives children an opportunity to act out feelings and fears. A small girl's cat was killed by an automobile. Her first reaction was one of shock and dismay, followed by outrage against her parents.

She felt they were guilty because they had not taken proper care of the pet. Yet her anger toward her parents was a substitute for her own guilt, for she had on occasion wished to be rid of "that awful pest." The child insisted that one of her favorite toys be buried with the cat. The toy served as a kind of peace offering to the "offended" pet. She was then relieved of anxiety and could continue to function effectively in her everyday activities. Rituals like this combine the dynamics of guilt, assuagement, and reparation, and are similar to the mourning behavior of adults. If a classroom pet dies, a teacher might suggest that the children plan and carry out some kind of burial.

Do not rush out too quickly to find a substitute for a dead animal. Let your children understand that the particular pet cannot be duplicated. Another collie may be purchased, but it will be different from the original one. Animals are not identical any more than human beings are. Wait for the youngsters to mourn their loss. If you desire another pet, you might purchase one that is slightly different and give the new animal a different name. Do not rob your children of the right to grieve, cope with, and overcome their pain.

National Tragedies

"My child and I were watching the space shuttle Challenger. *How excited we were with the lift off! Then came the explosion! I quickly switched to 'Sesame Street.'"*

You may change a television channel, but you cannot protect children from the knowledge and experience of world events. When a disaster is so sudden and unexpected, an entire country is shaken up. Children are curious to know what has occurred. They hear the news broadcasts, discuss the calamity in class, and talk it over with their friends.

The shuttle explosion touched the lives of many young people. Next to a child's parents, teachers play the most significant role in the lives of their students. In fact, Christa McAuliffe had planned to give classes in space. When the shuttle exploded, the jubilance of a seemingly perfect takeoff was suddenly replaced with sadness. Every child who watched was a witness to seven deaths. For people of all ages, the explosion and death were real and tragic.

The program "20/20" featured a segment called "Children's Fears," in which the astronaut's deaths were linked to the assassinations of the Kennedys and Martin Luther King, Jr. Death was graphically depicted as a part of life, along with children's disbelief, anger, guilt, and sadness. Youngsters saw the pain on the faces of the astronauts' families. They realized that the astronauts were not only heroes, but individuals with families of their own. Childhood illusions of safety were abruptly taken away. Many youngsters became anxious about any kind of separation from their parents, whether that involved parents' being late home from the workplace or a business trip. An entire nation mourned together.

When children hear of a public tragedy, they need to learn the facts from caring adults in simple, direct language. They should be able to express whatever emotions they may have—feelings of fear, physical distress, depression, or hostility. After the shuttle disaster, many were aided in their painful acceptance of the reality by their drawings and letters to the families of the astronauts. In situations such as this, there is always the need for parents' holding and touching with comfort, warmth, and love.

Fred Rogers of "Mr. Rogers' Neighborhood" had a special program for the assassination of President Kennedy that wonderfully addressed the parents:

> The best thing in the world is for your children to be included in your family ways of coping with the problems that present themselves anytime. But particularly now, in this very difficult time, in our nation. There are those who will find a great comfort in being able to sit and watch a television mass, or a funeral—so long as it is included in the family, this I feel is extremely appropriate. For other families, maybe a walk by a river, a walk in a favorite place. For others, maybe just a strong arm around the body of a small child as you walk.

Thoughts on Seeking Professional Help

"My daughter is taking her father's death so terribly. Maybe I should send her to a psychiatrist. She cries and cries and doesn't seem to care about anything."
"When did your husband die?"
"Two days ago."

Of course the daughter is taking her father's death "terribly." Death is a terrible thing for anyone. She has every right to grieve. However, it is not the time to panic and think the person is mentally ill.

When should you seek some kind of counseling? Certainly you may not be in a position to make a decision in the period immediately following death. At this time, it is very difficult to separate the normal from the distorted. Many people say and do things during crises that are not in keeping with their usual behavior. Grief and sorrow leave imprints upon the healthiest of personalities.

The line of separation between normal and distorted mourning reactions is thin indeed, like the division between normal and neurotic actions of any kind. The difference is not in the symptom itself, but in its intensity, for example, *continued* denial of reality even many months after the funeral; *prolonged* bodily distress; *persistent* frenzy; *extended* guilt; *unceasing* apathy; or *enduring* hostile reaction to the deceased and to others. In other words, each manifestation does not in itself indicate a distorted grief reaction; that can only be determined when such signs of mourning are viewed within the total framework of the person's behavior.

The question is not *how* is the child acting, reacting, or overreacting but for *how long*. After an initial period of mourning, children are often able to work themselves back to some degree of productive and near-normal living. After several months have elapsed, danger signals may be present if children continue to:

- look sad all the time and experience prolonged depression

- keep up a hectic pace and cannot relax the way they used to with you and their friends

- not care about how they dress and look

- seem tired, or unable to sleep, with their health suffering markedly

- avoid social activities and wish to be alone more and more

- be indifferent to school and hobbies they once enjoyed

- experience feelings of worthlessness and self-incrimination

- rely on drugs and/or alcohol

- let their moods control them instead of controlling their moods.

If you have doubts, do not hesitate to seek advice from a therapist, psychiatrist, psychologist, or child guidance clinic. (See the section "Reaching Out for Further Help," p. 83). There are times when even the best-informed and well-intentioned parents are simply inadequate. Getting professional assistance is not an admission of weakness but a demonstration of real love and strength.

Afterword: Coping with Adult Grief

This book is not just for children. It is also for you. What you are will determine what you teach youngsters. Your attitudes are being absorbed by your children. If you are unable to talk about death, they too will probably remain silent. If you conceal your emotions, they too may repress their fear, guilt, and confusion. In short, adults as well as children must face the fact that death *is* a part of life.

This is easier said than done. Your loved one is dead. It is final and irrevocable. You have feelings of sorrow, anxiety, and uncertainty about the future. You can't help thinking: "If only I had had a few more hours with him or her. If only I had treated that person a little bit better." You keep remembering all the things you wanted to say and do but didn't. Now it is too late.

Your friends may try to help you, but often their efforts are in vain. There is little consolation in knowing that countless others have suffered similar losses. You boil inside when people tell you how well you are doing. How do they know the flood of emotions that torments you? The ridiculous clichés—"It's all for the best" "It's God's will" "She lived to a ripe old age"—do not bring a healing balm when the pain of separation seems unbearable. When you hear the oft-repeated phrase, "I know just how you feel," you want to scream, "No, you don't! How could you possibly know how I really feel?"

You are in a state of shock. How do you accept the unacceptable? You are overwhelmed with self-pity, self-doubt, estrangement from people, and loneliness. Your feelings are frozen as you go through your daily activities mechanically. You are anxious and insecure about the future. "What will happen to me?"

Do you feel better if you cry? "Certainly not in front of the children," you say. Why not? Your secure, well-ordered world has crumpled. Release your feelings; don't bottle them up. Emotions should be accepted for what they are. Do not engage in a family cover-up campaign. How terrible it would be to have no emotions.

Life is not "fair"; you must find a way of living in an unfair world. You continue to exist. It is not like before; it is not the way you would decide if you had a choice. There are times when you are not sure that it is all worth it. You may wish you were dead. You may feel as though you are losing your mind. Yet you continue to survive. You are confronted with the seemingly bitter fact that you are destined to go on living. In the words of Edna St. Vincent Millay: "Life goes on . . . I forget just why."

Then somehow you begin to take yourself in hand. You accept the consolation and love of your family and friends. You learn the sad truth that many people do not wish to hear of your continuing grief. If, however, you have one close friend with whom you may share your feelings, you are truly fortunate. You are not alone. There are many fine organizations (see "Reaching Out for Further Help," p. 83) that can assist you when your so-called good friends have left the cemetery. There are also books (see "Additional Reading, Viewing, and Listening," p. 99) that can provide you with new insights.

You continue to ask, "Why did this happen to me? The funeral is over, but I am not getting any better. Who says that time heals?" There is a silent, knifelike terror that keeps recurring. You are grieving not only for the person who died but for yourself and your sense of loss. You keep telling yourself that you *must* face life without your loved one.

Psychologists call this approach "withdrawing the emotional capital of the past." You do not disregard the person who died. Memories should never be forgotten. But you realize that yesterday with its joys and sorrows has ended. All that it holds for your life is in the treasure house of the past. There are beautiful reminiscences—sweet and tender. They are yours, but now they are memories.

An effective way to break disabling ties with the past is by refusing to create a memorial shrine. Certainly, pictures and mementos can be retained as a visual, tangible reminder of days gone by. It is not necessary, however, to keep the person's clothes intact in the closet (in the secret hope that the individual will someday return). It is in the best humane tradition to give clothing to the Salvation Army, Good Will Industries, the homeless, or any organization dedicated to relieving the plight of the poor and needy. (A word of caution: you may wish to make donations to someone in the immediate vicinity, yet it can be a shocking experience to witness a neighbor in your loved one's clothes; you may think you are seeing a ''reincarnation'' of your loved one.) Furniture may also be rearranged. The goal is to strike that delicate balance between the past that should be remembered and a future that must be created.

As the weeks go by, the depth of your sorrow diminishes slowly and at times imperceptibly. You are doing things you never thought possible. You are discovering hidden capabilities you had never before tapped. You are growing in many ways. You are able to make decisions once again. You are withdrawing your dependence, declaring your independence, and planning for the future.

Later, your mind begins to recover from its numbed state. You seek new interests, satisfactions, creative activities. You experiment with undeveloped talent and potential. Perhaps you will begin the music lessons you always wanted to take . . . or enroll in classes . . . or take up the hobby you had always wished you could master.

Feelings are marvelously released through artistic media. One mother provided finger paints for her son so he could express his mood. The two worked together, talking as they painted. The mother later remarked that the hour was as helpful for her as for her child. One man expressed his feelings by playing pieces with crashing chords and dissonances on the piano.

Another way of coping is through physical activity: working in the garden, playing tennis, golf, walking, or jogging. (Of course, you should make sure you have a medical checkup before engaging in a strenuous sport.)

There are organizations, clubs, hospitals, charities, church, and civic groups that desperately need your help and talents. What a meaningful way to take your mind off yourself and your own anxieties. New relationships are formed, new acquaintances made, new challenges developed. At first, you may have to force yourself to leave the security of your home. Later, you lift up your own spirits as you lend a hand to another.

One danger. Some, in the desperate search for distraction at any cost, become involved in the headlong flight into endless activity. This frenzy offers only a temporary relaxation of tension. The effort becomes abortive, for you soon grow weary from physical fatigue and disenchanted with sporadic causes. Remember, any medicine taken to excess becomes a poison.

You will find that you occasionally need to be by yourself. Solitude is not necessarily loneliness. It is good to have time to think and take stock of your life. In solitude you cry and remember, but you also dream and hope. Since life is no longer the same, you formulate new philosophies of life. Self-awareness leads to understanding and recognition of your best potential. Grief is a strange mixture of joy and sorrow—joy at being alive, and sorrow at having life diminished by the loss of the one you love.

Just when you think you are making great strides forward and are coping well, you receive a startling setback. You think you are back at the point when your loved one just died. Realize that difficulty is not the same as defeat. Progress is almost always slow. You will have slips and spills before your footing becomes firmer; but slowly, slowly you will rebuild your world.

The most important gift you can give your children at this time is the feeling that life continues despite pain. Death, "the loss of innocence," can either lead you to the edge of the abyss and threaten your existence with meaninglessness and futility, or you can start to build the bridge that spans the chasm with the things that still count—memory, family, friendship, love. When you have sorted out your own feelings, you will be better able to understand your troubled children, who come to you laden with questions and beset with fears. This is the reason why this book is not solely for children. It is for you, the parents, as well. The real challenge is not just how to explain death to children, but how to make peace with it yourself.

Guidelines for Bereaved Adults

- *Accept your grief*
  Expect the physical and emotional consequences of the death of your loved one. Grief is the price you pay for love.

- *Accept your feelings*
  Don't mask your despair. Cry when you have to; laugh when you can.

- *Be patient with yourself*
  Your mind, and body, and soul need time and energy to mend.

- *Monitor your health*
  Eat as well as you can, for your body needs nourishment after the physically grueling experience of grief. Depression can also be lightened by biochemical changes through proper exercise. Put balance back into your life through work and relaxation. Have a complete checkup and tell the physician about the loss in your life.

- *Avoid the abuse of alcohol and drugs*
  Drugs and alcohol can sedate for the moment but ultimately can leave the nervous system in shreds. Drugs alter the normal process of grief work, conceal legitimate emotions, and create destructive problems.

- *Share your pain with a friend or friends*
  Don't withdraw from others. By your silence, you deny them the opportunity to share your inner self. Ralph Waldo Emerson wrote: ''A friend is a person with whom I may be sincere.''

- *Join a group of others who are grieving*
  Learning about the experiences of others can offer invaluable insights into your own feelings and provide support, encouragement, and friendship.

- *If you are religious, you might seek solace from your faith*
  Even if you ask, "How could God allow this to happen?" sorrow can be a spiritual pilgrimage. Religion is something you may wish to use— not lose—during your bereavement with a wisdom that has nourished souls of humankind for untold generations. Just remember that grieving intensely is not an indication of a weak faith.

- *Help others*
  By devoting your energies to people and causes, you learn to relate to others better and face reality by living in the present. As Edwin Markham wrote, "Only the soul that knows the mighty grief can know the mighty rapture."

- *Do what has to be done, but delay major decisions*
  Begin with little things—a single chore that has to be accomplished. That can help restore your confidence. But wait (if you can) before deciding to sell your house or change jobs. Thomas Carlyle said: "Our main business is not to see what lies dimly at a distance but to do what lies clearly at hand."

- *Determine to live again*
  Readjustment does not come overnight. Try to put the stars back into your sky. Hold on to hope and don't give up. Resolve to survive each new day.

Resources

Reaching Out for Further Help

Death is separation and pain, anger and grief. It is learning to live without the familiar face and smile of a loved one. How will it be possible to survive those long, vacant hours when the longing will not go away? Part of you has been buried with the one who died.

Usually there is family and community support during the first weeks. Then friends may assume that you and your children have adjusted to your new life and that your grief is now past. After all, the funeral is over and the flowers have withered. Everything should be back to normal. Yet this is when the sense of loss is most intense and you are most alone. You and your children may feel adrift, drowning in the sea of your private sorrow.

Your family will not be able to handle the emotional impact of loss until *you* deal with the fact that the loss has occurred. There is no getting around pain; the only cure for grief is to grieve. Mourning is a process, not a state, and it requires "grief work." You and your children may need to verify that you are not "crazy" and what you are experiencing is normal.

Helping hands come in many forms—friends, family, professional counseling, support groups, and "bibliotherapy" with books that can help you to understand your turmoil. If you will only reach out during these horrifying moments of stress and adjustment, help can be on the way. You need not be alone in your grief.

Helpful Professional and Referral Agencies

CLERGY

Not all clergy have been trained in crisis intervention. You may contact someone who is experienced in working with loss through:

American Association of Pastoral
 Counselors
3 West 29th Street
New York, N.Y. 10001

The Canadian Association for Pastoral
 Education
P.O. Box 96
Roxboro, Que. H8Y 3E8
Canada

GUIDANCE AND FAMILY ASSOCIATIONS

American Association of Marriage and
 Family Counselors
225 Yale Avenue
Claremont, Calif. 91711

Child Welfare League
404 First Street, N.W.
Washington, D.C. 20001
 This caring organization is mobilized to help children in crisis.

Family Service Association of America
44 East 23rd Street
New York, N.Y. 10010
 The association conducts a major program of family counseling for child care and personal development. Its purpose is to enable families to help themselves.

National Association for Mental Health
1800 North Kent Street
Arlington, Va. 22209
 A national volunteer citizens' organization working through state associations to combat mental illness and promote mental health.

National Association of Social Workers
7981 Eastern Avenue
Silver Springs, Md. 20910

National Council on Family Relations
1219 University Avenue, S.E.
Minneapolis, Minn. 55414
 Founded in 1938 as an interprofessional forum through which members of many disciplines work and plan together to strengthen family life.

Canadian Mental Health Association
880 Ouellette Avenue, Suite 901
Windsor, Ont. N9A I27
Canada
 This organization includes bereavement specialists.

Psychological and Psychiatric Services

Below are three major national associations with accredited professionals and services:

American Psychological Association
1200 17th Street, N.W.
Washington, D.C. 20036

American Psychoanalytic Association
1 East 57th Street
New York, N.Y. 10022

American Psychiatric Association
1700 18th Street, N.W.
Washington, D.C. 20009

Other Organizations

A variety of groups are dedicated to helping children and their families deal with grief.

The American National Red Cross
National Headquarters
Washington, D.C. 20006

National Association for Death
  Education and Counseling
638 Prospect Avenue
Hartford, Conn. 06104
  An organization devoted to the promotion and upgrading of the quality of death education and counseling.

Barr-Harris Center
The Institute for Psychoanalysis
180 North Michigan Avenue
Chicago, Ill. 60601
  The thrust of their work is the study of separation and loss during childhood, especially as it affects youngsters under ten years of age.

Big Brothers of America
220 Suburban Station Building
Philadelphia, Pa. 19103

Big Brothers of Canada
18 Glouchester
Toronto, Ont. M4G 3Z9
Canada
  With hundreds of local member agencies, Big Brothers has helped thousands of boys who have no father with whom to identify.

Big Sisters of America
220 Suburban Station Building
Philadelphia, Pa. 19103
  This group is especially recommended for the widower who feels that his daughter should have the companionship of an older female volunteer.

85

Center for Death Education and
  Research
University of Minnesota
1167 Social Science Building
Minneapolis, Minn. 55455

The Center is involved in all aspects of death, grief, and bereavement and disseminates materials to both professionals and the general public.

Foundation for Thanatology
630 West 168th Street
New York, N.Y. 10032

An educational and scientific organization sponsoring workshops and symposia for professionals; it also publishes many relevant books on death.

United Way of America
801 North Fairfax Street
Alexandria, Va. 22314

The Information and Referral Service helps bereaved parents and children find an appropriate agency.

Department of Public Health
64 Merton Street
Toronto, Ont. M4S 1A1
Canada

Public health nurses monitor the health of the bereaved while encouraging them to talk about their feelings.

Helpful Support Groups

Support groups are based on the philosophy that bereavement is a psychologically healthy and normal state. Through the mutual help provided by the peer group, they facilitate the mourning process and prevent the serious effects of unresolved grief.

The list of support groups is not inclusive. Many communities have support groups that have been formed at the local level. These groups may have been formed by a particular church, synagogue, hospital, or social service agency. Many groups are formed to meet the needs of a specific population. Be sure to check with your community mental health agency or crisis and information center for a complete listing of support groups in your area.

SCHOOLS

Many schools recognize the needs of bereaved students to meet in a safe, secure environment with others who are grieving for a parent, sibling, friend, or significant other.

The Centre for Living with Dying
554 Mansion Park Drive
Santa Clara, Calif. 95054

The Centre has an extensive educational program for students, teachers, staff, and parents, as well as a carefully trained Healing Heart Speakers Bureau. When a death occurs in a school population, they design special assemblies to acknowledge and deal with the loss. "Follow-up support groups or ceremonies allow for the expression of subsequent feelings, reactions, unfinished business, and saying goodbye in an uplifting, healing way."

Good Grief Program
Judge Baker Guidance Center
295 Longwood Avenue
Boston, Mass. 02115

The Good Grief Program

• provides crisis intervention to schools and community groups to help children and adolescents when a friend is terminally ill or dies.

• Offers consultation to teachers, administrators, group leaders, parents and others about ways to respond to the needs which arise when a friend of the group is terminally ill or dies.

• Trains staff selected by schools and community groups to assist these groups in developing their own capacity to respond to groups of bereaved children and adolescents.

• Prepares and distributes resource materials including annotated bibliographies of books and films for use with children.

• Maintains a resource library of films, books, and other materials which may be borrowed by schools and groups that have used the Good Grief Program.

• Assists schools and community groups in enlisting the help and support of resources that can assure the continuation and success of the program.

The program is replicated in other parts of the country to help students "at risk" because of a recent death or terminal illness of a friend or family member.

HELPFUL CLUBS AND ORGANIZATIONS FOR BEREAVED CHILDREN

The Dougy Center
P.O. Box 66461
Portland, Oreg. 97266

A support center to help grieving children and their families by meeting in an atmosphere of trust, acceptance, and unconditional love.

Fernside, A Center for Grieving
    Children
P.O. Box 8944
Cincinnati, Ohio 45208

The Center offers peer-group support to children and their families who are mourning the loss of a loved one.

Rothman-Cole Center for Sibling Loss
1456 West Montrose Avenue
Chicago, Ill. 60613

The focus of this organization is on sibling bereavement and how to help surviving children cope with their loss and to grow intellectually, emotionally, and socially.

T.I.G.E.R. (Teens in Grief: Educate, Rebuild, Support)
521 Garden Court
Quincy, Ill. 62301

A base of support to educate young people in the grieving process and to comfort them in a loving and caring way.

SCHOOL COUNSELORS

When there is a death in the family, children may regress and seem "out of it." Inform the school so teachers will understand the child's possible changing behavior. The school environment often becomes the focus of children's grief.

Most communities have a coordinated counseling service for students from kindergarten level through high school. Counseling is the core of a guidance department. Inform the department of the death in the family and the way in which your youngsters seem to relate to the loss. The counselor may help identify emotional difficulties, if any, that can adversely affect both educational development and mental health. Through personal interviews, contact with teachers, and appropriate testing, the guidance department can help the youngsters toward self-understanding in meeting their special needs. Referrals to professional agencies may be in order if circumstances warrant.

HELPFUL SUPPORT FOR BEREAVED PARENTS

When a Child Dies

In *Understanding Bereavement and Grief* Ann Kliman writes: "Parents who lose a child are multiply victimized. We are victimized by the realistic loss of the child we love, we are victimized by the loss of dreams and hopes we had invested in that child, and we are victimized by the loss of our own self-esteem. Not unlike survivors of concentration camps, we cannot comprehend why we did not die instead."

In a 1988 study among bereaved parents at the University of California, San Francisco, it was learned that family members experienced a sense of "empty space" for at least seven to nine years after the child's death. (These findings conflict with traditional bereavement theories, which claim that grief is usually resolved after two years.) The study uncovered three distinct patterns for grieving: *getting over it, filling the emptiness,* and *keeping the connection.* Those families who actively tried to *keep the connection* most frequently felt what the researchers call the "empty space" phenomenon, but all the families experienced it occasionally, even after almost a decade.

The following support groups can help both bereaved parents and surviving children.

The Compassionate Friends
P.O. Box 3696
Oak Brook, Ill. 60521

Compassionate Friends of Canada
Les Amis Compatissants du Canada
685 William Avenue
Winnipeg, Manitoba R3E OZ2
Canada
The Compassionate Friends is an international group (United States, Canada, Australia, South Africa, the Netherlands, Israel, and Switzerland) for bereaved parents that encourages family members, especially siblings, to share in the task of mutual support.

Bereaved Parents
1717 South Puget Sound
Tacoma, Wash. 98405

First Sunday
3977 Second Avenue
Detroit, Mich. 48201

St. Francis Hospital
North Road
Poughkeepsie, N.Y. 12601

When a Spouse Dies

Widows, widowers, and their children are too often overlooked as they face the greatest challenge in their lives. Recognizing the special needs of the newly bereaved, Dr. Phyllis R. Silverman, a psychiatric social worker, and Dr. Gerald Caplan of the Laboratory of Community Psychiatry of Harvard Medical School, started the Widow-to-Widow Project in 1967. Its emphasis is on self-help groups in which the primary caregiver is another widowed person. The concern and goal are to stimulate programs of preventive intervention for widow, widower, and their children.

Widow/widower programs have grown nationwide; the following are but a random sample of such organizations:

Widowed Persons Service (WPS)
1909 K Street, N.W.
Washington, D.C. 20039

The National Retired Teachers Association, the American Association of Retired Teachers, and Action for Independent Maturity (NRTA-AART-AIM) jointly form a network for living through bereavement. An outreach program helps those on a one-to-one basis as well as those in larger group sessions, with a telephone service for referral information, a public education program for family adjustment, and counseling for financial and legal affairs. Trained volunteers who have themselves been widowed two years or more have learned through their own experiences to reach out by listening, sharing, socializing, and providing useful materials for sorting out practical details of insurance, social security, and estate planning.

THEOS Foundation
717 Liberty Avenue, Suite 1301
Pittsburgh, Pa. 15222

THEOS Foundation
Willowdale Chapter

Trinity Presbyterian Church
2737 Bayview Avenue
Willowdale, Ont. M24 1C5
Canada

An organization for widowed and their families, THEOS is an acronym meaning *They Help Each Other Spiritually. Theos* is also the Greek word for God, since many chapters meet in houses of worship.

Bereaved Families of Ontario
Les Familles endeuillées d'Ontario
33 Bloor Street East, Suite 210
Toronto, Ontario M4W 3HI
Canada

Center for New Directions
51 Jefferson Avenue
Columbus, Ohio 43215

COPE
425 Senate Avenue
Delaware, Ohio 43105

Connecticut Council—Widows
 Widowers Associated
60 Lorraine Street
Hartford, Conn. 06105

Maria Stein Center
Young Widowed Support Group
2365 St. Johns Road
Maria Stein, Ohio 45860

National Association for Widowed
 People
P.O. Box 3564
Springfield, Ill. 62708

Widowed Information and Consultation
 Services
223 North Yakima Avenue
Tacoma, Wash. 98403

Widowed Persons Association of
 California
2628 El Camino Avenue, Suite D 18
Sacramento, Calif. 95821

Widows and Widowers (With School-
  Age Children)
467 Brevoort Road
Columbus, Ohio 43124

Widows Consultation Center
136 East 57th Street
New York, N.Y. 10022

There is also an international organization with over a thousand affiliates that is devoted to single parents and the interests of their children.

Parents without Partners
7910 Woodmont Avenue, Suite 1000
Washington, D.C. 20014

Special Kinds of Death

AIDS

When AIDS patients die, survivors have very special needs because of intense emotional reactions. They may feel they have failed as spouses or parents or lovers. They may feel guilty because they abandoned their loved one in the greatest hour of need. They may feel angry because of the person's nontraditional life-style. They may even feel that they are the victims of retributive justice—that God has used the illness to punish sinful behavior. Mostly the survivors feel helpless and alone.

AIDS survivors desperately need help in understanding their emotions. They need friends who will listen and love and not be judgmental. Children especially need to know that they are not at risk, because AIDS is not contagious through casual contact. Ignorance and intolerance need to be replaced with facts and compassion through proper education. They need warmth and affection as well as understanding. They also need to know that there are community resources that will help them through their agonizing crisis.

AIDS Support Group
8119 Holland Avenue
Alexandria, Virginia 22306

American Red Cross
AIDS Public Education Program
(contact local chapter for information)

American Association of Physicians for
  Human Rights
(M.D. referrals)
P.O. Box 14366
San Francisco, Calif. 94114

Fund for Human Dignity
(Educational material)
(212) 741-5800

National Association of People with
    AIDS
(202) 493-3708

National Gay and Lesbian Crisis Line
(Crisis counseling)
(800) 221-7044

National Hemophilia Foundation
Soho Building
110 Green Street, Room 206
New York, N.Y. 10012

National Lesbian and Gay Health
    Foundation
P.O. Box 65472
Washington, D.C. 20035

DRUNK DRIVER VICTIMS

Each year drunken drivers kill or seriously injure thousands of innocent people. Families and friends must live with the aftermath of their horrifying loss. Support groups for victims are often co-led by another victim and a professional. Together they express their loneliness, bitterness, confusion as they work through their feelings of anguish.

In addition to supporting families and friends, these groups work to convince the community that impaired driving is not only socially unacceptable but illegal as well. Aggressive campaigns are being waged in individual states to pass tough drunk driving laws.

The destructiveness of drunk driving is most effectively dramatized by MADD (Mothers Against Drunk Driving). MADD was created by Candy Lightner, whose thirteen-year-old daughter was killed in 1980 by a repeat offender in Fair Oaks, California. She and her group have become "the voice of the victims." Not only do they provide information about victim rights under state law, MADD is also in the forefront in advocacy groups when criminal justice fails to deal adequately with the perpetrator.

In addition to the more than 400 MADD chapters in the United States, other groups have created their own networks, which include Students Against Driving Drunk and Bartenders Against Drunk Driving.

MADD (Mothers Against Drunk
    Driving)
669 Airport Freeway, Suite 310
Hurst, Tex. 76053

RID (Remove Intoxicated Drivers)
P.O. Box 520
Schenectady, N.Y. 12301

SADD (Students Against Driving
   Drunk)
P.O. Box 800
Marlborough, Mass. 01752

PRIDE
19 Ovida Avenue
Islington, Ont. M9B 1E2
Canada

SURVIVORS OF HOMICIDE

Grief is especially complicated when a loved one has been murdered. There are intense psychological reactions for the survivors of a homicide. The Victims Services Agency in New York City describes the grief in this way: "In working with families of homicide victims, we have learned that homicide inflicts a devastating emotional trauma on the surviving relatives. Among the reactions we typically encounter are: shock and apathy; helplessness and terror; overwhelming rage; guilt; intense yearning for the one who is dead. . . . For the survivors, murder of a loved one is often compounded by isolation and increased loneliness."

After a child is murdered, husband and wife may grieve in different ways. One may blame the other for allowing those circumstances where the victim was vulnerable. There is an extremely high divorce rate among couples who have experienced the violent death of a child, as if the situation could be remedied by starting over with someone else without painful memories and reminders.

The entire family may be barraged by inquiring reporters by prolonged media coverage. Often it is perceived that the offender is glorified while the suffering family must live with their horrible loss. The judicial process is a nightmare that renews the tragedy. The verdict may be considered too lenient and in some cases the so-called guilty person is not even sentenced.

Children, too, feel depressed and alienated when a loved one has been murdered. They may act out their unresolved grief by dropping out of school, or using alcohol or drugs to ease their pain.

Friends, family members, and professionals such as clergy, police, hospital personnel, teachers, and therapists may not realize the effects of violent death. Often they tell the bereaved that "they are doing so well" even though they are experiencing inner agony and an overpowering urge for revenge.

Parents of Murdered Children (POMC) was formed for the families of those who have died by violence. Often siblings attend the group meetings, or there may be special chapters for them. Conferences and workshops are held to discuss:

- *Funeral service/autopsy* (survivors often encounter "second victimization" when the body of the homicide victim is examined to determine the cause of death)

- *Coping with grief*

- *Police* (usually the family's first contact with the criminal justice system)

- *Prosecutor/trial* (the point at which survivors may question whether there is any justice for the victim's family)

- *Wrongful death actions/civil suits* (what can be done apart from the criminal justice process)

- *Marital problems*

- *Victims' rights* (the head of the National Organization for Victim Assistance provides the latest information)

- *Starting and running a chapter of POMC*

- *Coordinating with the local victim/witness program*

It must be emphasized that healing after murder is a lifelong process.

POMC (Parents of Murdered Children)
100 East Eighth Street, Room B-41
Cincinnati, Ohio 45202

Families and Friends of Missing
  Persons and Violent Crime Victims
P.O. Box 27529
Seattle, Wash. 98125

Families and Friends of Murder Victims
P.O. Box 80181
Chattanooga, Tennessee 80181

National Organization for Victim
  Assistance (NOVA)
717 D Street, N.W.
Washington, D.C. 20004

Victims of Violence
P.O. Box 393
Boulton, Ont. L7E 1A0
Canada

Some children's deaths are explainable: that is, there are names for the cause—accident, leukemia, meningitis. But there is one kind of death for which there is no precise cause. The medical term is Sudden Infant Death Syndrome (SIDS).

The clinical definition of SIDS is "the sudden death of any infant or young child which is unexpected by history, and in which a thorough postmortem examination fails to demonstrate an adequate cause of death." In other words, despite the use of an official-sounding word like *syndrome*, the cause of death remains unexplained.

More than one-third of the deaths of babies aged one week to one year fall into this category; more die of SIDS than from congenital birth defects, diseases of early infancy, influenza, pneumonia, or accidents. The current United States rate is about two babies per 1,000 live births. From 7,000 to 10,000 apparently healthy babies die mysteriously every year.

One of the most notable aspects of SIDS is that it occurs in apparently healthy, normal, thriving babies who almost always have received skillful and loving care. It does not reflect on the ability of the parents to care for their child. Many theories about the cause of such deaths have been proposed and then discarded. Current theories now under investigation include spasm of the larynx, heart failure due to stoppage in breathing, and defects in the infant's immunological or nervous system. The fact remains, however, that at this time there is no way either to predict or prevent Sudden Infant Death Syndrome.

The universal reaction of parents who lose a baby under such circumstances is the question, "Was it my fault?" They must be assured that there is no way to prevent or foretell death on the basis of present knowledge. Death in these infants is sudden, almost instantaneous in most cases. Parents must be reassured that their baby did not suffer. A careful and thorough autopsy is sometimes of value in alleviating parents' feelings of guilt and self-blame. Usually the examination reveals no disease sufficient to account for the death.

SIDS is not contagious; it cannot be passed to others. Nor is it hereditary. A couple need not worry about having subsequent children, for

SIDS is *seldom repeated* in the same family. The real danger is the psychological damage to both parents and surviving children.

Because of its characteristic suddenness, SIDS catches parents completely unprepared to deal with the death. Disbelief is the initial reaction. Parents often speak of the infant in a combination of present and past tenses.

Guilt is universal and pervasive. Parents dwell on the last feeding, harboring doubts about what they did or neglected to do. They wish they had taken the baby to the doctor, particularly if the infant had a cold. If the child *was* seen by a physician they wonder "what the doctor missed."

Children are deeply affected by the death of an infant sister or brother. They may harbor feelings of anger and jealousy because the baby consumed the parents' time and attention, and older siblings may have wished that the infant would "go back to the hospital where she was born and leave them in peace." Now that the baby is gone, they may believe that their wish caused the death.

It is important to tell children immediately about the death of the infant. Explain that the baby died of SIDS and that no one is to blame. Reassure them that SIDS is rare and happens only to infants. Be careful not to say that "the baby went to sleep." Because the baby brother or sister may have died while asleep, the surviving children may become confused and fearful that they too will die at bedtime.

Help them to accept the reality of their loss. Be sensitive to their reactions. Be aware of their fears and fantasies. Assist them to reinvest their energies in everyday activities so they can learn to love and trust again.

Because of the uncertainties surrounding Sudden Infant Death Syndrome, parents and children may feel abandoned and alone. Support and information are readily available from SIDS and other organizations.

National Sudden Infant Death
  Syndrome
8200 Professional Place, Suite 104
Landover, Md. 20785

The National Clearinghouse for SIDS
8201 Greensboro Drive, Suite 600
McLean, Va. 22102

Council for Guilds for Infant Survival
P.O. Box 3841
Davenport, Iowa 52808

Counseling and Research Center for
Sudden Infant Death
1700 West Wisconsin Avenue
P.O. Box 1997
Milwaukee, Wis. 53201

Pregnancy Loss Support Network
70 Lincoln Way, East
Jeannette, Pa. 15644

Pregnancy and Infant Loss Center
1415 East Wayzata Boulevard, Suite 22
Wayzata, Minn. 55381

SHARE
St. Elizabeth's Hospital
211 South Third Street
Belleville, Ill. 62222

Canadian Foundation for the Study of
Infant Death
586 Eglinton Avenue East, Suite 308
Toronto, Ont. M4P 1P2
Canada

SIDS Network Newsletter
873 Crowells Street
Oshawa, Ont. L1X 1X8
Canada

SUICIDE SURVIVORS

Suicide is not a neutral word; it evokes apprehension and creates a desire to avoid or detach oneself from further discussion. When suicide occurs, it evokes powerful reactions. The impact of a suicide is felt emotionally, physically, intellectually, and spiritually.

In many cities and towns, there are self-help organizations for families and friends of suicides. They share their feelings and experiences and gain strength through association with others who are surviving. Slowly and positively, they will begin to heal and reconstruct their lives. As one support organization says, "We've been helped. We want to help you."

American Association of Suicidology
2459 South Ash
Denver, Colo. 80222

Friends for Survival, Inc.
5701 Lerner Way
Sacramento, Calif. 95823

Lifeline Institute [for youth suicide]
9108 Lakewood Drive, S.W.
Tacoma, Wash. 98499

National Committee on Youth Suicide
Prevention
230 Park Avenue, Suite 835
New York, N.Y. 10169

National Save-A-Life League
4520 Fourth Avenue, Suite MH3
New York, N.Y. 11220

Omega [a support group for families of
    suicides]
271 Washington Street
Somerville, Mass. 02143

Samaritans
500 Commonwealth Avenue
Boston, Mass. 02215

Suicide Research Unit
National Institute of Mental Health
5600 Fishers Lane, Room 10C26
Rockville, Md. 20857

Survivors of Suicide—National Office
Suicide Prevention Center, Inc.
184 Salem Avenue
Dayton, Ohio 45406

Survivors of Suicide
c/o Advent Christian Church
905 East Edgelawn
Aurora, Ill. 60506

Survivor Support Programme
10 Trinity Square
Toronto, Ont. M4G 1B1
Canada

The following quarterly newsletter is
highly recommended:

*Afterwards: A Letter For and About Suicide
    Survivors*
c/o Adina Wrobleski, Editor
5124 Grove Street
Minneapolis, Minn. 55436

If there are other groups or organizations that you believe should be
included in this section, please contact the author at the following
address:

Dr. Earl A. Grollman
c/o Beacon Press
25 Beacon Street
Boston, Massachusetts 02108-2800

Local Support Groups

Name _____

Address _____

City, state, zip _____

Phone _____

Contact person _____

Outreach or focus of group _____

Additional Reading, Listening, and Viewing

The Treatment of Death in Children's Literature

Examine a child's book dealing with death and you will quickly understand how the concept of separation was viewed by the adult world at the time the book was written.

Many years ago death was a customary aspect of life. Because of the high mortality rate, early literature alluded to death with an almost obsessive frequency. In modern times, this attitude was replaced by an unhealthy avoidance of the inevitable. Fortunately, in past years there has been a noticeable change. The subject of death and dying has become a respectable concern for the health professional and social scientist. Instead of pretending that death is not a basic condition of life, the theme of death is now included in the curricula of hundreds of elementary grades, high schools, and universities. Children's writers are not only talking about the biological processes surrounding the beginning of existence, they are beginning to discuss the reality of the end of the life cycle as well. These new resources display a maturity of spirit that not only understands the purpose of life but accepts the mystery of death. Since the last edition of this book, another hundred new reference volumes have appeared, including books on AIDS and other topics not previously discussed.

A word of caution. Before you direct your child to a book from the following list you should read the book yourself. Do you think that the concepts in the book will confuse your child? Should the book be about a dead animal or a real person? Who is the individual who has died? A grandparent, parent, sibling, or friend? Did the person die of natural causes or by accident? Is the main character of the story a boy or girl with whom your child could identify? To better aid you in your selection, a brief description follows each recommended book.

The age categories for the bibliography are meant to serve only as a general guide. For example, E. B. White's *Charlotte's Web* has been placed in the fiction section of the library for the middle grades, yet many have found it ideal for a read-aloud to fairly mature seven- to eight-year-olds. There are, of course, developmental differences even for youngsters of the same age, so take time to decide which books may be most useful. Just as your children learn about life from the books they read, they can also learn about death, which is the other part of life.

Preschool to Age Eight

Bartoli, Jennifer. *Nonna.* New York: Harvey House, 1975. Through patience and understanding, a young boy learns to accept the death of his grandmother.

Brown, Margaret W. *The Dead Bird.* New York: Young Scott Books, 1958. In finding a dead bird whose body is still warm, a little girl and her playmates encounter death for the first time.

Burns, Maureen, and Cara Burns. *Life and Death in the Third Grade.* Greenville, Mich.: Empey Enterprises, 1988. A third-grader's abrupt thrust into the world of death through the sudden accident of a close friend.

Carrick, Carol. *The Accident.* New York: Seaberg Press, 1976. An honest look at a young boy's feelings of anger, guilt, and depression after his dog is killed.

De Paola, Tomie. *Nana Upstairs and Nana Downstairs.* New York: G. P. Putnam's Sons, 1973. A quiet story of the wonderful times that Tommy shares with his great-grandmother (Nana Upstairs) and his grandmother (Nana Downstairs). Each dies, but lives on in memories.

Dobrin, Arnold. *Scat.* New York: Four Winds Press, 1971. When Scott's Grandma dies, Scott heeds her final advice to "listen to what your heart says . . . not your head." He says good-bye to her by playing the blues on his harmonica.

Fassler, Joan. *My Grandpa Died Today.* New York: Behavioral Publications, 1971. A tender story of a love shared by a young boy and his grandfather. When the grandfather dies, the boy is comforted when he realizes that despite his pain, he has "to go right on playing and reading, and running, and laughing, and growing up."

Harris, Audrey. *Why Did He Die?* Minneapolis: Lerner Publications, 1965. A small child wrestles with the concept of his grandfather's death.

Hickman, Martha. *Last Week My Brother Anthony Died.* Nashville: Abingdon Press, 1984. A young girl talks about missing her brother, who died when he was a month old. Recommended especially for those families who have experienced the loss of an infant.

Hogan, Bernice. *My Grandmother Died.* Nashville: Abingdon Press, 1983. A boy misses his grandmother after her death but is comforted by familiar reminders of her presence, such as a pair of green mittens and larkspur in the backyard.

Kantorwitz, Mildred. *When Violet Died.* New York: Parent's Magazine Press, 1973. Violet, a parakeet, dies. A youngster learns that nothing lasts forever, but there is comfort in the continuity of life exemplified by the children's pregnant cat.

Lawrence, Melinda. *For Everyone I Love.* Alexandria, Va.: Children's Hospice International, 1987. A tender, true story of a young girl with muscular dystrophy whose courage brought inspiration to the founder of Children's Hospice International.

Martin, Patricia M. *John Fitzgerald Kennedy.* New York: G. P. Putnam's Sons, 1974. A picture book of the life and death of the former president. There is a particularly vivid account of the assassination and funeral. Very popular with second- to fourth-graders for reading on their own.

Mellonie, Byron, and Robert Ingpen. *Lifetimes.* New York: Bantam Books, 1983. Plants, animals, and people all have a lifetime, so dying is as much a part of living as being born.

Miles, Miska. *Annie and the Old One.* Boston: Little, Brown, 1971. A beautiful story of a little American Indian girl who is given a weaving stick by her dying grandmother.

Smith, Doris. *A Taste of Blackberries.* New York: Crowell, 1978. In this Child Study Association Award–winning book, a boy struggles with his own grief when his best friend dies as a result of an allergic reaction to a bee sting.

Stein, Sara. *About Dying.* New York: Walker Books, 1974. This book contains two versions of the text—one for children and one for adults. The children's version includes the death of a pet bird and then of a grandfather and shows how one can cope with each loss.

Thomas, Ianthe. *Hi, Mrs. Mallory.* New York: Harper Books, 1979. A young girl has a very special relationship with a neighbor, Mrs. Mallory, and explores her reactions when Mrs. Mallory dies suddenly.

Viorst, Judith. *The Tenth Good Thing about Barney*. New York: Atheneum, 1971. When Barney the cat dies, his young owner tries to think of ten good things to say at the funeral.

Warburg, Sandol S. *Growing Time*. Boston: Houghton Mifflin, 1979. After Jamie's dog dies, the young boy finally begins to accept the loss with the help of his understanding family.

Williams, Margery. *The Velveteen Rabbit*. Garden City, N.Y.: Doubleday, 1971. Thought-provoking story about life and death from the vantage point of a toy rabbit.

Zolotow, Charlotte. *My Grandson Lew*. New York: Harper, 1974. Before the story begins, Lew's grandfather has died. Lew misses Grandpa, whose "beard scratched" when he kissed and who would comfort Lew after a bad dream. What makes the story so touching is the loving relationship in which the small child can share his memories with his mother.

MIDDLE GRADES: AGES EIGHT TO ELEVEN

Alcott, Louisa M. *Little Men*. New York: Macmillan, 1963. Thirteen boys make Plumfield House ring with the sounds of laughter and tears. In the afterword, Clifton Fadiman writes, "The most moving episode has to do with John Brooke's death and funeral. As I read it, I found myself wondering why most books for children these days are afraid to mention death."

———. *Little Women*. New York: World, 1969. Generations of young people have had their first vicarious experience with death and grief through *Little Women*. In the classic story of New England life in the early 1900s, Beth, one of the four March sisters, dies, surrounded by her dear ones. The family is very real, the death is very real, and the effects it has on the survivors are treated skillfully. Especially popular with fourth- to eighth-grade girls.

Beim, Jerrold. *With Dad Alone*. New York: Harcourt, Brace, 1954. In this story it is the mother who dies. The boy must now assume some new duties, such as helping with his younger brothers.

Brandenberg, Aliki. *The Two of Them*. New York: Greenwillow Books, 1979. A lovely description of the love of a grandfather and a girl in the markings of time—life and death. She cares for him when he is sick and remembers him fondly when he dies.

Buscaglia, Leo. *The Fall of Freddie the Leaf*. New York: Holt, Rinehart and Winston, 1982. A story about how Freddie the leaf and his companions change with the seasons and ultimately fall to the ground with winter's snow. A touching allegory about the balance between life and death.

Buck, Pearl S. *The Big Wave*. New York: John Day, 1947. When Jiya's parents die in a tidal wave, his foster father, with wisdom and tenderness, helps him to accept the tragedy.

Center for Attitudinal Healing. *There Is a Rainbow Behind Every Dark Cloud*. Berkeley, Calif.: Celestial Arts, 1979. Through pictures and words children talk about how they come to terms with terminal illness.

Chin-yee, Fiona. *Sam's Story*. Halifax, Nova Scotia: Project Sam Publishing, 1988. A wonderful story told from the child's viewpoint about a family surviving Sudden Infant Death Syndrome.

Cleaver, Vera, and Bill Cleaver. *Grover*. Philadelphia: J. B. Lippincott, 1970. Eleven-year-old Grover's dying mother has shot and killed herself. Is it an accident? In a burst of rage, Grover takes revenge by killing a turkey, but finds no relief. Finally, after experiencing terrible pain, he begins to mature and face life.

Coburn, John B. *Anne and the Sand Dobbies*. New York: Seabury Press, 1964. "This is the story about my sister, Anne, who died. It's also the story of Bonnie, my dog, who died too—or rather got killed." With the help of an adult friend and mythical sand dobbies, a boy reaches an understanding of what it means to die.

Cohen, Barbara. *Thank You, Jackie Robinson*. New York: Lothrup, Lee and Shepard, 1974. Twelve-year-old Sam and the elderly black cook, Davy, both share a deep interest in sports, especially in the late Jackie Robinson. When Davy suffers a fatal heart attack, the reader identifies and sympathizes with Sam's intense feelings of grief.

Corley, Elizabeth A. *Tell Me about Death, Tell Me about Funerals*. Santa Clara, Calif.: Grammatical Sciences, 1973. A child learns of the intricate details of what happens when his grandfather dies. What is a funeral home, an embalmer, casket, pallbearer, hearse, mausoleum? His parents comfort him: "You miss him very much, but you can still think about him and you can still love him."

Coutant, Helen. *First Snow*. New York: Alfred A. Knopf, 1974. A six-year-old Vietnamese girl learns the meaning of death when her grandmother shows her the new-fallen snow. The drops of water have not disappeared but changed into a new form of existence.

Cunningham, Julia. *Wings of the Morning*. Los Angeles: Golden Gates Junior Books, 1981. A young girl encounters her first death experience—a "sleeping bird" in the park.

Greene, Constance. *Beat the Turtle Down*. New York: Viking, 1976. A narration about the happiest week in a girl's life until her sister falls off a horse and dies.

Kipling, Rudyard. *The Jungle Book.* Garden City, N.Y.: Doubleday, 1964. Mowgli, lost in the jungle of India as a baby, is brought up by wolves and becomes an integral part of the animal life around him. A description of the impartial law of nature.

L'Engle, Madeleine. *Meet the Austins.* New York: Vanguard Press, 1960. Maggy, a child orphaned when her father is killed in a plane crash, comes to live with the Austins. She is insolent and sullen. Eventually Maggy accepts the loss, aided by the warmth and security of the Austin family.

Linn, Erin. *Children Are Not Paperdolls.* Greely, Colo.: Harvest Printing, 1982. Drawing and comments by bereaved children which can be used to strengthen communication between youngsters and their families.

Mann, Peggy. *There Are Two Kinds of Terrible.* New York: Doubleday, 1977. A story about how a young boy faces the death of his mother and must learn to relate to his withdrawn and sorrowful father.

Patterson, Francine. *Koko's Kitten.* New York: Scholastic, 1985. A wonderfully documented relationship between a cat and a gorilla, about life and grief.

Patterson, Katherine. *Bridge to Terabithia.* New York: Corwell, 1977. Newberry Prize Award–winner which tells the story of a friendship between a boy and girl and an ensuing tragedy.

Richter, Elizabeth. *Losing Someone You Love.* New York: Putnam, 1986. Young people share their experiences about the death of their sibling.

Tobias, Tobi. *Petey.* New York: Putnam, 1978. A girl confronts the death of a pet gerbil, experiencing anger, sadness, and then fond memories.

Vogel, Ilse-Margaret. *My Twin Sister, Erika.* New York: Harper and Row, 1986. A girl tells of the sorrowful loss of her twin sister and of finding relief in sharing feelings of sadness, loneliness, and guilt with her mother. Appropriate to any brother/sister loss.

White, E. B. *Charlotte's Web.* New York: Harper and Row, 1952. An animal fantasy. When Charlotte, the spider, dies at the fair grounds, her friends, Templeton the rat and Wilbur the pig, manage to take her eggs back to the farm where they can safely hatch. For reading to six- to eight-year-olds, or for eight- to twelve-year-olds to read to themselves.

Whitehead, Ruth. *The Mother Tree.* New York: Seabury Press, 1971. The story of a ten-year-old girl whose mother dies suddenly. She now has to help with the household chores as well as take care of her clinging four-year-old sister, who continually asks, "When will Mother be home again?" A moving experience of how the girls spend the summer with their grandmother.

Windsor, Patricia. *The Summer Before.* New York: Harper and Row, 1973. A journal of an adolescent girl's reactions to her boyfriend's accidental death. Through therapy, she accepts the situation and looks forward to the future.

Zim, Herbert S., and Sonia Bleeker. *Life and Death.* New York: William Morrow, 1970. In a straightforward manner the writers discuss the physical facts, customs, and attitudes surrounding death. Funeral and burial procedures are described and compared with those of other cultures.

Age Twelve and Up

Agee, James. *A Death in the Family.* New York: Avon, 1959. The Pulitzer Prize–winner describes death as an inseparable part of the human experience. A novel of overwhelming sensitivity and compassion about how a family and a six-year-old boy, Rufus Follet, respond to the death of a father.

Blume, Judy. *Tiger Eyes.* New York: Dell, 1981. A girl must cope with the murder of her father and put her life together.

Brown, John M. *Morning Faces.* New York: McGraw-Hill, 1949. Various sketches describe the excitement, disappointment, surprises, and joys of being the parents of two small boys. The chapter "The Long Shadow" is about an eleven-year-old boy who asserts, "I don't like God anymore . . . why should I? Now that He has done this to my father." The conclusion is that, though death is final, memories have a life of their own.

Buck, Pearl S. *The Good Earth.* New York: John Day, 1931. In an almost pastoral style, the book beautifully describes the cycle of birth, marriage, and death in a Chinese peasant family during the early twentieth century.

Cleaver, Vera, and Bill Cleaver. *Where the Lilies Bloom.* Philadelphia: J. B. Lippincott, 1969. After the death of both of her parents, a fourteen-year-old Appalachian girl helps her three siblings struggle to survive a long, bitter winter. In a moving tribute to human endurance, the children manage to stay together and help one another.

Coerr, Eleanor. *Sadako and the Thousand Paper Cranes.* New York: Putnam, 1977. A true story of a young girl who dies as a result of leukemia caused by the atomic bombing of Hiroshima.

Crane, Stephen. *Red Badge of Courage.* New York: Random House, 1951. The personal reactions of a young recruit during the Civil War. Henry Fleming soon learns the meaning of battle and death. Soldiers are less often motivated by unselfish heroism than by fear and egoism.

Craven, Margaret. *I Heard the Owl Call My Name*. Garden City, N.Y.: Doubleday, 1973. With three years to live, a twenty-seven-year-old Anglican missionary is sent to an Indian village in Canada. He finally comes to understand the real meaning of life and death.

Dooley, Thomas A. *Doctor Tom Dooley, My Story*. New York: Farrar, Strauss, 1960. The personal account of Dr. Dooley before his death at the age of thirty-four. "The jagged, ugly cancer scar went no deeper than my flesh. There was no cancer in my spirit."

Frank, Anne. *The Diary of a Young Girl*. New York: Washington Square Press, 1963. A moving autobiography of a twelve-year-old Jewish girl who lives with seven other people in an Amsterdam attic during the Nazi occupation. Anne died, but her diary lives.

Grollman, Sharon. *Shira: A Legacy of Courage*. New York: Doubleday, 1988. The inspiring biography of a courageous child's coming to terms with her own dying and of the reactions of her family, friends, and community.

Hemingway, Ernest. *A Farewell to Arms*. New York: Charles Scribner's Sons, 1929. Hemingway combines austere realism and poetic language with a moving story of war, love, and death.

Hoffman, Alice. *At Risk*. New York: G. P. Putnam's Sons, 1988. Love triumphs over heartbreak in the story of an eleven-year-old girl with AIDS.

Holland, Isabelle. *Of Love and Death and Other Journeys*. New York: Lippincott, 1975. A fifteen-year-old girl's struggle for acceptance by her father after her mother's death.

Klein, Norma. *Sunshine*. New York: Avon, 1974. Based on the real-life diaries and tapes of a dying nineteen-year-old youth.

Krementz, Jill. *How It Feels When a Parent Dies*. New York: Alfred A. Knopf, 1981. Sensitive text and photographs of interviews with eighteen young people from ages seven to sixteen as they reveal their sadness and courage following the death of a parent.

L'Engle, Madeleine. *A Wrinkle in Time*. New York: Farrar, Straus and Giroux, 1962. A science-fiction story of good versus evil and life versus death. Three children pass through time and defeat "IT" with their chants of love.

LeShan, Eda. *Learning to Say Goodbye*. New York: Macmillan, 1976. In simple, direct language the author discusses the questions, fears, and fantasies that children may have about a parent who has died.

Lutters, Valerie. *The Haunting of Julie Enger*. New York: Atheneum, 1977. A broken-hearted young girl finds comfort after her father's death by frequenting the places that they once enjoyed together.

Miller, Arthur. *Death of a Salesman.* New York: Viking Press, 1949. The story of Willy Loman blends the themes of social and personal tragedy. His downfall and final defeat illustrate not only the failure of a man but also the failure of a way of life.

Mohr, Nicholasa. *Nilda.* New York: Harper and Row, 1973. A very personal story of a twelve-year-old Puerto Rican girl surviving ghetto life in New York City. Sad, funny, fascinating, and honest in its description of life and death as seen through a child's eyes.

Mumford, Lewis. *Green Memories.* New York: Harcourt, Brace and World, 1947. Geddes, the son of the author, was killed in World War II when he was nineteen. An insight into the heart of a loving and bereaved parent.

Rofes, Eric. *The Kids' Book about Death and Dying.* Boston: Little, Brown, 1985. A child-to-child perspective on death in which young people between the ages of eleven and fourteen share their understanding and experiences.

Rudowsky, Colby. *What About Me?* New York: Watts, 1976. The story of a teenager and her handicapped brother whom she often wishes out of existence. The handling of this conflict and of the brother's death makes for fascinating reading.

Schotter, Roni. *A Matter of Time.* New York: Philomel, 1979. A social worker helps a sixteen-year-old girl accept the death of her mother and grow through her painful experience.

Scivani, Mark. *Love, Mark.* Syracuse: Hope for the Bereaved, 1980. A magnificent set of handwritten letters for grieving youth will help them gain insights into how to live through their pain.

Stoltz, Nancy. *By the Highway Home.* New York: Harper and Row, 1979. A thirteen-year-old girl's adjustment to her brother's being killed in Vietnam.

Talbert, Marc. *Dead Birds Singing.* Boston: Little, Brown, 1985. The story of a seventh-grader's turmoil when a drunken driver kills her mother and sister.

Selected Adult Volumes about Death and Children

Anthony, Sylvia. *The Child's Discovery of Death.* New York: Harcourt Brace, 1940. Anthony is one of the first authors to have made a comprehensive study of the subject of children and death based on direct observation of school children. She based her interpretation on the Freudian principle that, to a child, death means little more than departure or disappearance. She maintains that consciousness of death develops with the intellect rather than on the basis of chronological age.

Bernstein, Joanne. *Books to Help Children Cope with Separation and Loss.* New York: R. R. Bokder, 1977. A bibliographic treasure to help children through loss and separation.

———. *Loss and How to Cope with It.* New York: Seabury, 1977. Addressed to older children and adults who are trying to cope with loss.

Bluebond-Langer, Myra. *The Private Worlds of Dying Children.* Princeton, N.J.: Princeton University Press, 1978. A cultural anthropologist's remarkable observations of children with leukemia in a hospital pediatric ward.

Cook, Sarah, ed. *Children and Dying.* New York: Health Sciences, 1974. The book is divided into two sections: how children feel and react to death, and how adults react to the sick, dying, or bereaved child.

Corr, Charles, and Joan McNeal, eds. *Adolescence and Death.* New York: Springer, 1986. A comprehensive exploration of the ways youth face dying, death, and bereavement.

Deits, Bob. *Life after Loss.* Tucson: Fisher Books, 1988. A thought-provoking and encouraging approach for successful recovery from painful losses.

DiGiulio, Robert C. *Beyond Widowhood.* New York: Free Press, 1988. A book that will help those who are widowed and others to gain insight into the process from bereavement to hope.

Donnelly, Katherine Fair. *Recovering from the Loss of a Sibling.* New York: Dodd Mead, 1988. This book of hope and healing provides a valuable communication tool for bereaved parents and surviving children.

Fargues, Marie. *The Child and the Mystery of Death.* Glenn Rock, N.J.: Dews Books, 1966. Written under the auspices of the Paulists in France, Madame Fargues's book is a lucid blending of modern psychology and Catholic education concerning the child's understanding of the mystery of death. Included are discussion questions for teachers and clergy.

Gaffney, Donna. *The Seasons of Grief: Helping Your Children Grow through Their Loss.* New York: New American Library, 1988. A helpful book for both parents and professionals with important advice on helping children grow through crisis.

Grollman, Earl A. *Concerning Death: A Practical Guide for the Living.* Boston: Beacon Press, 1974. Contributing essays by experts on the practical aspects of death and its aftermath.

———. *Explaining Death to Children.* Boston: Beacon Press, 1967. Outstanding specialists in guidance, psychology, and religion offer their recommendations to ease a child's confrontation with death.

———. *In Sickness and in Health.* Boston: Beacon Press, 1987. Emotional guidance for parents and children during the crisis of sickness and dying.

———. *Living When a Loved One Has Died.* Boston: Beacon Press, 1987. Straightforward, gentle thoughts to help the grieving go on living after the death of a significant other.

———. *Suicide: Prevention, Intervention, Postvention.* Boston: Beacon Press, 1987. How to recognize the warning signs of a potential suicide, how to intervene when a suicide has been attempted, and how to comfort the family after a life has been taken.

———. *Time Remembered: A Journal for Survivors.* Boston: Beacon Press, 1987. A combination of comforting passages and a journal for the reader's own entries.

Gullo, Steven. *Death and Children.* New York: Dobbs Ferry, 1985. A guide from many perspectives for educators, parents, and children.

Jackson, Edgar N. *Telling a Child about Death.* New York: Channel Press, 1965. A rare combination of honesty, simplicity, and profound respect for human dignity in telling a child about death. Jackson covers such questions as when and how to talk about death and what to say to children of different ages.

Kübler-Ross, Elisabeth. *On Children and Death.* New York: Macmillan, 1983. A compassionate book to help the dying child and the family during the time of unmanageable grief.

Kushner, Harold. *When Bad Things Happen to Good People.* New York: Schocken, 1981. The acclaimed best-seller that continues to bring spiritual comfort to the millions of people who have suffered a loss.

Lester, Andrew. *When Children Suffer.* Philadelphia: Westminster Press, 1976. Written as a sourcebook for clergy, the book can help all who work with children face the crises of life and death.

Lewis, C. S. *Of Grief Observed.* New York: Seabury, 1961. Personal observations of how the famous author's life changed after his wife's death.

Linzer, Norman, ed. *Understanding Bereavement and Grief.* New York: Yeshiva University Press, 1977. Social workers, clergy, medical personnel, funeral directors, and therapists discuss the psychological aspects of the death of a loved one, ceremonial observances, and special problems of widows, widowers, and bereaved parents and children.

Lonetto, Richard. *Children's Conceptions of Death.* New York: Springer, 1980. A detailed, graphic developmental guide to youngsters' understanding of death between the ages of three and twelve.

Mace, Gillian. *The Bereaved Child.* New York: Plenum, 1981. An abstracted bibliography of over 550 citations of children's reactions to the death of parents, siblings, friends, teachers, pets, and even presidents.

Manning, Doug. *Don't Take My Grief Away*. New York: Harper and Row, 1984. A practical and consoling guide for those who have experienced a death in the family.

Mitchell, Marjorie E. *The Child's Attitude to Death*. New York: Schocken, 1967. When a child becomes aware of death, emotional reactions may be expressed in two simple sentences—"I don't want to die" and "I don't want you to die." The writer attempts to understand children's emotions from religious, scientific, and sociological points of view.

Rondo, Therese. *Grief, Dying, and Death*. Champaign, Ill.: Research Press, 1987. Theoretical and practical information for working with both those who are dying and those left behind.

Rudolph, Marguerita. *Shall the Children Know?* New York: Schocken, 1978. A testament to the strength and adaptability that children have in dealing with tragic situations.

Temes, Roberta. *Living with an Empty Chair*. New York: Irvington, 1980. A graphic guide on how to live through grief, including a wonderful section on children.

Vachon, Mary. *Occupational Stress in the Care of the Critically Ill, the Dying, and the Bereaved*. Washington, D.C.: Hemisphere, 1981. An illuminating book to help caregivers function through stress and distress.

Viorst, Judith. *Necessary Losses*. New York: Simon and Schuster, 1986. The loves, illusions, dependencies, and impossible expectations that must be surrendered in order to grow.

Wass, Hannelore. *Dying: Facing the Facts*. Washington, D.C.: Hemisphere, 1979. Provides perhaps the best basic background on dying and death.

Wass, Hannelore, and Charles Corr, eds. *Helping Children Cope with Death: Guidelines and Resources*. 2d edition. Washington, D.C.: Hemisphere, 1984. Excellent sourcebook for understanding specific problems faced by caregivers, terminally ill children, and their families.

Wass, Hannelore, R. A. Pacholski, and C. M. Sanders. *Death Education: An Annotated Guide*. Washington, D.C.: Hemisphere, 1980. An indispensable, comprehensive, annotated resource manual.

Wolf, Anna M. *Helping Your Child to Understand Death*. New York: Child Study Press, 1973. A revised edition of this classic offers new material on the effects on the young of mass-media violence, televised war, and upheavels in traditional religious and moral values. A former senior staff member of the Child Study Association of America, Wolf writes with understanding and compassion.

Bereavement: A Magazine of Hope and Healing. 350 Gradle Drive, Carmel, Ind. 46032 (nine issues per year).

Death and Life Newsletter. Brooklyn College Thanatology Program, Department of Health Science, Brooklyn, N.Y., 11210 (quarterly).

Death Studies (formerly *Death Education*). Hemisphere Publishing Company, 79 Madison Avenue, New York, N.Y. 10016 (quarterly).

Forum Newsletter. Association for Death Education and Counseling, P.O. Box 7782, Eugene, Oreg. 97401 (ten issues per year).

Journal of Palliative Care. University of Toronto Press, 63A St. George Street, Toronto, Ont. M5S 1A6, Canada (biannual).

Loss, Grief and Care: A Journal of Professional Practice. The Haworth Press, 12 West 32nd Street, New York, N.Y. 10001 (quarterly).

Omega: The Journal of Death and Dying. Baywood Publishing Company, 26 Austin Avenue, Amityville, N.Y. 11701 (quarterly).

Thanatos (a realistic journal for families as well as professionals). Florida Consumer Information Bureau, P.O. Box 6009, Tallahassee, Fla. 32314 (quarterly).

The Hospice Journal: Physical, Psychosocial, and Pastoral Care of the Dying. The Haworth Press, 12 West 32nd Street, New York, N.Y. 10001 (quarterly).

Recommended Films on Death and Dying

Film and television are two of the most powerful and pervasive media of our time. The following films are excellent introductions to discussions of death and dying. It is suggested that you preview each film to determine just how it can serve your audience. Determine in advance the questions that the film might raise and the insights you might present.

For Younger Children

And We Were Sad, Remember? 25 minutes, color. United States Division of Educational Technology, National Audiovisual Center, United States Office of Education, 400 Maryland Avenue, S.W., Washington, D.C. 20202.

A mother, father, and two young children react to the death of a grandmother. Conflict arises over what to tell the children about death. From the "Footsteps" television series on parenting.

Anna and Poppy. 16 minutes, color. Paulist Communications, 17575 Pacific Coast Highway, P.O. Box 1057, Pacific Palisades, Calif. 90272.

Ten-year-old Anna overcomes sadness at the death of her grandfather, Poppy, by remembering the warm and happy times they both spent together. A film designed to facilitate discussing death with young children, and which treats the subject with honesty and delicacy.

The Day Grandpa Died. 12 minutes, color; ISBN 0-699-069556. Kings Broadcasting Company, 320 Aurora Avenue, North Seattle, Wash. 98109.

When David learns of his grandfather's death, he rushes into the room screaming, "I don't want him dead." The setting is an upper-middle-class Jewish suburban home. There are flashbacks to memories of the happily shared activities of David and his grandfather.

Death of a Goldfish. 30 minutes, color. Program #231 in "Mister Rogers' Neighborhood." Family Communications, Inc., 4802 Fifth Avenue, Pittsburgh, Pa. 15213.

A dead fish is found floating on top of the water. Mr. Rogers tries to revive it but in vain. At the conclusion Mr. Rogers says, "It helps to say that you're sad, and if you feel like crying, cry, and if you feel like running around, then just run around. Each person is different."

The Dead Bird. 13 minutes, color. Indiana University, Audio-Visual Center, Bloomington, Ind. 47401.

Margaret Wise Brown's classic takes the form of cartoon pictures and voice-over narration to present the insights of children who discover, bury, and mourn for a dead bird.

The Death of a Friend: Helping Children Cope with Grief and Loss. 15 minutes, color. Judge Baker Program, Judge Baker Children's Center, 295 Longwood Avenue, Boston, Mass. 02115.

Two puppets discuss their fears and worries when their friend is killed by a car. The film helps children talk about the sadness, anger, and confusion they feel when a friend dies.

Gramp: A Man Ages and Dies. 16 minutes, color. Valley Film Works, 1010 Winola Road, Klarks Summit, Pa. 18411.

Based on the book *Gramp* by Mark and Dan Jury. Visual documentation and commentary of the gradual deterioration and death of an elderly man, and the family who loved and cared for him.

In My Memory. 14½ minutes, color. Inside/Out Series Film, National Instructional Television, Box A, Bloomington, Ind., 47401.

A young girl's response to the death of her grandmother. She cries: "Grandma left me alone; she didn't want to be with me anymore." Especially recommended for third- and fourth-graders.

Mr. Rogers' Special: Kennedy Assassination. 1 hour, black and white. Family Communications, Inc., 4802 Fifth Avenue, Pittsburgh, Pa. 15213.

A moving, poignant film on the death of Senator Robert Kennedy.

My Turtle Died Today. 5 minutes, color. BFA Educational Media, 2211 Michigan Avenue, Santa Monica, Calif. 90404.

Despite the combined efforts of a boy's father, teacher, and a pet store owner, a sick turtle dies.

Nine-Year-Olds Talk about Death. 15 minutes, black and white. International Film Bureau, 332 South Michigan Avenue, Chicago, Ill. 60604.

A group of fourth-graders shares their understanding of death and dying with a teacher who is off-camera.

Rabbit. 15½ minutes, color. Eccentric Circle Cinema Workshop, P.O. Box 1481, Evanston, Ill. 60204.

A good film for introducing children to the subject of death. At the outset a boy is faced with a dilemma of how to dispose of a family of rabbits which he has been told he may not keep. His decision concerning one of the rabbits leads to its death. When he discovers this, the boy is saddened and made to ponder the consequences of his act.

Talking about Death with Children. 13 minutes, color. Batesville Management Services, P.O. Box 90, Batesville, Ind. 47006.

Earl Grollman explores the subject of death and funerals with elementary school youngsters.

Uncle Monty's Gone. 16 minutes, color. University of Illinois, Visual Aids Service, 1325 South Oak Avenue, Champaign, Ill. 61820.

An entertainer dies but the children decide that the show must go on.

Understanding Death. Sound filmstrip series. Educational Perspectives Associates, P.O. Box 213, DeKalb, Ill. 60115.

For the middle-school student. Each filmstrip comes with accompanying teacher's guide. Filmstrips are from 50 to 65 frames in length; playing time, 12–15 minutes.

"Explaining the Cemetery": Burial, memorials, cremation are among the topics covered.

"Facts About Funerals": The filmstrip tells of a boy who visits a funeral home and then reports to the class on his findings.

"A Taste of Blackberries": Adapted from the book by Doris B. Smith about a young boy's best friend who dies suddenly.

"Children and Death": How to help children arrive at an understanding of death. A valuable resource for schools, churches, PTA sessions, and community organizations by David Berg and George Daugherty.

Where Is Dead? 19 minutes, color. Encyclopedia Britannica Educational Corporation, 425 North Michigan Avenue, Chicago, Ill. 60611.

A wonderful illustration of the dynamics of grief, mourning, and adjustment in the story of a six-year-old girl who learns to cope with the sudden death of her older brother.

For Older Children and Adults

AIDS Alert. 18 minutes, color. United Learning, 6633 West Howard Street, Niles, Ill. 60648.

The first cartoon video on AIDS for school systems with expert medical commentary.

All the Way Home. 103 minutes, black and white. Films Incorporated, 1144 Wilmette Avenue, Wilmette, Ill. 60091.

Based on James Agee's *A Death in the Family*, the film is not as concerned with the impact of death on a child as is the novel; still, a good film for older children and adults. Judith Crist writes: "Sensitivity and subtlety are indeed present and we are engrossed by time and place and people." For ages fourteen and older.

Brian's Song. 75 minutes, color. Learning Corporation of America, 1350 Avenue of the Americas, New York, N.Y. 10019.

A true story dramatized for television about the professional football player, Brian Piccolo, and the impact of his death from cancer at age twenty-six.

But He Was Only Seventeen. 35 minutes, color. Batesville Management Services, P.O. Box 90, Batesville, Ind. 47006.

Peer reactions to the sudden death of a seventeen-year-old youth who is killed in an automobile accident. A National Education Film Festival Finalist.

Children and Death. 15 minutes, color. Alan D. Wolfelt, Wolfelt Productions, 814 West Charles Street, Muncie, Ind. 47305.

An animated program that acquaints teachers and parents with the developmental stages of a child's understanding of death.

Cipher in the Snow. 25 minutes, color. Brigham Young University, Media Services, West 164 Stadium, Provo, Utah 94602.

A moving story of how family and friends began to appreciate a youth only after his death.

A Conference for a Dying Child. 44 minutes, black and white. Video Nursing, 2834 Central Street, Evanston, Ill. 60201.

A nurse's emotions in caring for a dying child. Discusses the support needed by the patient and family.

Dead Birds. 81 minutes, black and white. Audio-Visual Center, Indiana University, Bloomington, Ind. 47401.

An excellent cross-cultural approach to the life and customs of the Baliem Valley people of Western New Guinea. The film explores their death customs as well as other tribal traditions.

Death. 42 minutes, black and white. University of California, Extension Media Center, 2223 Fulton Street, Berkeley, Calif. 94720.

A documentary that reveals how poorly prepared most people are for the terror and isolation of dying. The film follows a fifty-two-year-old terminal cancer patient through his last days in a city hospital. Physicians discuss the psychology of dying and defenses of the dying person.

Death of a Gandy Dancer. 26 minutes, color. Learning Corporation of America, 1350 Avenue of the Americas, New York, N.Y. 10019.

A boy and his family face the dying of Grandfather Ben, who enthralls the youngster with memories of "gandy dancing" when railroad tracks were laid. A significant exploration of the importance of memory as a family dynamic.

The Diary of Anne Frank. 150 minutes, color. Films Incorporated, 1144 Wilmette Avenue, Wilmette, Ill. 60091.

Based on the classic autobiography of

Anne Frank, this is a portrayal of her adolescent years in the secret attic hideout in Amsterdam during World War II. Bosley Crowther of the *New York Times* wrote, "The magnificence of human endurance and compassion . . . shines in virtually every character."

Did Jenny Have to Die? 41 minutes, color. Batesville Management Services, P.O. Box 90, Batesville, Ind. 47006.

An in-depth analysis of a case of a pretty, bright, popular sixteen-year-old girl who commits suicide. Students view the details of this tragedy through the eyes of family members, friends, teachers, and of the victim herself.

Epitaph: The Lingering Heart. 25 minutes, color. WKYC-TV, Public Affairs Department, 1403 East Sixth Street, Cleveland, Ohio 04414.

A study of a wife and daughter's grief and readjustment when a young husband and father dies of leukemia.

Eric's Story: Walk in the World for Me. 19 minutes, color. Batesville Management Services, P.O. Box 90, Batesville, Ind. 47006.

The true story of Eric Lund, told by his mother, Doris Lund. Eric, a young man twenty-one years old, fights to enjoy life while facing death.

A Family in Grief: The Amache Story. 26 minutes, color. Group II Productions, 1 East 24th Street, Baltimore, Md. 21218.

Reactions, thoughts, and feelings of the Amache family to the death of their twenty-two-year-old son and brother.

Forbidden Games. 90 minutes, black and white. Janus Films, 745 Fifth Avenue, New York, N.Y. 10022.

A little girl is orphaned when the Nazis strafe a column of fleeing refugees. Amid the chaos of war, she and a little boy with whose family she comes to live build a "play cemetery" in which they bury dead animals dragged from the battlefields. In French with English subtitles; for ages fourteen and older.

Gift of Life/Right to Die. 15 minutes, black and white. University of California, Extension Media Center, 2223 Fulton Street, Berkeley, Calif. 94720.

What happens when a patient is dying and another patient desperately needs one of the dying person's organs? Physicians cite ideas on euthanasia and engage in discussions on medical ethics and other controversial situations.

How Could I Not Be among You? 29 minutes, color. Eccentric Circle Cinema Workshop, P.O. Box 1481, Evanston, Ill. 60204.

Portrait of a poet who is about to die and knows it. Ted Rosenthal had leukemia and had about six months to live. Filmed during his last months, the picture captures the agony and hopes of a gifted young man. For ages sixteen and up, this film has been widely hailed by medical and educational professionals.

How Do You Explain Death to Children? 28 minutes, color. Walter J. Klein Company, 6301 Carmel Road, Charlotte, N.C. 28222.

This film with Earl Grollman helps teachers, parents, and youths better understand the feelings of young people who face the death of a loved one.

I Never Sang for My Father. 92 minutes, color. Macmillan Audio Brandon, 34 MacQuesten Parkway South, Mt. Vernon, N.Y. 10550.

The death of a wife leaves a tyrannical older man in conflict with his middle-aged son. Death causes various identity problems.

I Never Saw Another Butterfly. 15 minutes, color. Macmillan Films, 34 MacQuesten Parkway South, Mt. Vernon, N.Y. 10550.

A film record of children's drawings from a Nazi concentration camp depicting their hopes, fears, and anticipation of death.

Jocelyn. 28 minutes, color. Canadian Broadcasting Corporation, P.O. Box 500, Terminal A, Toronto, Ont. Canada.

A beautiful, spiritual film of a seventeen-year-old who explains what is important to her as she faces a life-threatening illness.

The Last Full Measure of Devotion. 27½ minutes, color. National Funeral Directors Association, 1121 West Oklahoma Avenue, Milwaukee, Wis. 53227.

The highlights of the John F. Kennedy funeral and the emotional impact of his death as compared with the ceremonies for Lincoln and Franklin Roosevelt.

Last Rites. 30 minutes, color. Filmmaker's Library, 133 East 58th Street, Suite 703, New York, N.Y. 10022.

A young boy retreats into fantasy because he cannot accept his mother's death; finally he receives help from a stranger who teaches him to accept the bitter reality.

Lasting Memories: United States Presidents. 26 minutes, color. Batesville Management Services, P.O. Box 90, Batesville, Ind. 47006.

A historically informative exploration of Americans working through grief for their leaders who were tragically assassinated.

Living—When a Loved One Has Died. 19 minutes, color. Batesville Management Services, P.O. Box 90, Batesville, Ind. 47006.

This program by Earl Grollman explains many of the normal reactions individuals may experience in dealing with the pain of grief. It also suggests ways to cope with the feelings of depression, guilt, and anger so that one can work toward a new life.

Love Story. 100 minutes, color. Films Incorporated, 1144 Wilmette Avenue, Wilmette, Ill. 60091.

Film production of Erich Segal's bittersweet novel about the love of Oliver Barrett IV and Jenny Cavilleri. Jenny dies at the age of twenty-five and Oliver and his estranged father become reconciled.

My Grandson Lew. 13 minutes, color. Barr Films, Box 5667, 3490 East Foothill Boulevard, Pasadena, Calif. 91107.

Based on the book by Charlotte Zolotow, this film raises questions about when, how, and what to tell children about a death in the family.

An Occurrence at Owl-Creek Bridge. 28 minutes, black and white. Visual Aids Service, University of Illinois, Division of University Extension, Champaign, Ill. 61822.

The dramatization of Ambrose Bierce's short story about an incident in the Civil War. A young Southerner about to be hanged for sabotage manages to escape when the rope breaks. Death, however, is not an abstraction but a reality as he contemplates the real meaning of life. For ages fourteen and up.

One in 350; Sudden Infant Death. 30 minutes, black and white. National SIDS Foundation, Room 1904, South Michigan Avenue, Chicago, Ill. 60604.

Parents share their innermost emotions when their children die of Sudden Infant Death Syndrome.

Perspectives on Death. Sound filmstrip series. Educational Perspectives Associates, P.O. Box 213, DeKalb, Ill. 60115.

For the high school student, the program consists of four components: an audiovisual package containing two color-sound films and two separate tape cassette presentations, an anthology of readings, a student activity book, and a teacher's resource book. The audiovisual package includes the following:

"Funeral Customs Around the World": A 110-frame color filmstrip with cassette narration, exploring funeral customs around the world.

"Death through the Eyes of the Artist": How the artist has attempted through style, color, subject matter, and symbolism to capture the mood of death.

"Death Themes in Literature": Authors, poets, and dramatists bring their literary insights to an understanding of death.

"Death Themes in Music": Musicians express their emotions through classical, jazz, folk, and modern music.

Designed as a six-week mini-course that can be incorporated into the existing English or social studies program.

Richie. 31 minutes, color. Learning Corporation of America, 1350 Avenue of the Americas, New York, N.Y. 10019.

An edited selection from the film *The Death of Richie,* this film describes a teen-ager's drug addiction and its effect upon the family.

Suicide. 13 minutes, color. Batesville Management Services, P.O. Box 90, Batesville, Ind. 47006.

Based on Earl Grollman's book *Suicide—Prevention, Intervention, Postvention,* this film presents recollections and personal advice of a youth who attempted suicide.

The Syndrome of Ordinary Grief. 32 minutes, color. University of Texas Medical Branch, Videotape Library of Clinical Psychiatric Syndromes, Galveston, Tex. 77550.

A medical student describes his reactions to the accidental death of his only child.

Teens Who Chose Life: The Suicidal Crisis. 45 minutes, color. Batesville Management Services, P.O. Box 90, Batesville, Ind. 47006.

This film explores the special dynamics of adolescent suicide, using the moving stories of three teenagers who attempted suicide and survived.

Things in Their Seasons. 79 minutes, color. Learning Corporation of America, 1350 Avenue of the Americas, New York, N.Y. 10019.

A portrayal of the dynamics of dying and death on a dairy farm in Wisconsin when a family member is diagnosed with leukemia.

A Time to Live . . . A Time to Die. 39 minutes, color. Batesville Management Services, P.O. Box 90, Batesville, Ind. 47006.

A psychologist helps a young woman work through her father's sudden death.

Understanding Grief: Kids Helping Kids. 14 minutes, color. Batesville Management Services, P.O. Box 90, Batesville, Ind. 47006.

Earl Grollman's film designed for young people aged nine to fourteen. Children were interviewed who experienced the death of a loved one or a pet, with the emphasis on *talk, touch, tears,* and *time.*

Until I Die. 30 minutes, color. Associated Sterling Films, 600 Grand Avenue, Ridgefield, N.J. 07657.

Dr. Elisabeth Kübler-Ross describes her work with the terminally ill and conducts interviews with patients.

When Parents Grow Old. 15 minutes, color. Learning Corporation of America, 1350 Avenue of the Americas, New York, N.Y. 10019.

For junior and senior high school students, as well as college students. Faced with the problems of a suddenly widowed father whose health is failing, a young man on the verge of marriage must decide where his responsibilities lie. The film explores the problem of responsibility to aging parents and society's treatment of the elderly.

When Your Loved One Is Dying. 16 minutes, color. Batesville Management Services, P.O. Box 90, Batesville, Ind. 47006.

A program written by Earl Grollman for hospices, hospital personnel, parents, teachers, and youths to help them understand terminal illness and the dying process.

Widows. 43 minutes, black and white. Mental Health Training Film Program, Harvard Medical School, 33 Fenwood Road, Boston, Mass. 02115.

Widows discuss the deaths of their husbands, their grief, and the kinds of help they found useful.

Why Study Death. 18 minutes, color. Batesville Management Services, P.O. Box 90, Batesville, Ind. 47006.

An informative death education class that talks about the questions and concerns of the young.

You See, I've Had a Life. 32 minutes, black and white. Eccentric Circle Cinema Workshop, P.O. Box 1481, Evanston, Ill. 60204.

A thirteen-year-old boy is stricken with leukemia. As the story unfolds, each hospital visit leaves him closer to his untimely death. Fortunately, he has a family who, instead of hiding the illness, share the final meaningful experience of death. For ages fourteen and older, senior high or college, adult groups, and mental health associations.

The Young Man and Death. 16 minutes, color. Macmillan Films, 34 MacQuesten Parkway South, Mount Vernon, N.Y. 10550.

Death as viewed through the arts, with the theme explored through ballet and the music of Bach.

Your Biological Guide to AIDS. 18 minutes, color. Films Incorporated, 5547 North Ravenswood Avenue, Chicago, Ill. 60640.

This BBC production provides insightful visuals with a candid text for senior high school students.